Methuen Notes
Study-aid Series

Notes on Shakespeare's
HENRY IV
PART 2

Compiled by **M. Arkin,** Ph.D.

Methuen Paperbacks Ltd

First published 1978 by Methuen Paperbacks Ltd
11 New Fetter Lane, London EC4P 4EE
Reprinted 1978
Copyright © Cyril Kemp 1978
Filmset in Great Britain by Northumberland Press Ltd,
Gateshead, Tyne & Wear
Made and printed in Great Britain
by Richard Clay (The Chaucer Press) Ltd,
Bungay, Suffolk

ISBN 0 417 20610 0

All rights reserved.
No part of this publication may be reproduced,
stored in a retrieval system, or transmitted
in any form or by any means, electronic,
mechanical, photocopying, recording or otherwise,
without the prior permission of the publisher.

Note
These Notes are published for use as an aid to the
study of English Literature for examination purposes.
It is important to remember that the Notes serve only
as an aid to the study of the book and do not in any
way relieve the student of the necessity of reading
the original text.

Contents

I	Shakespeare's place in English literature	page 1
II	Suggestions on reading Shakespeare	7
III	General introduction to the play	9
IV	The historical background	12
V	Brief outline of the plot	17
VI	Summary of the play	20
	Act one	20
	Act two	23
	Act three	26
	Act four	28
	Act five	33
VII	Shakespeare's dramatic style	37
VIII	Characterization	40
IX	Revision exercises	55
X	Bibliographical note	58

1 Shakespeare's place in English literature

William Shakespeare was christened in the prosperous market-town of Statford-on-Avon, Warwickshire, on 26 April, 1564; traditionally, his actual birthday was three days earlier, on St George's Day, the same day as his death fifty-two years later. His father, John, was a respected middle-class trader, and his mother, Mary Arden, came from a family of local landowners. It seems probable that young William received a fair education at the local Grammar School, being well-grounded, as was then the custom, in the Latin classics and the art of Rhetoric, or effective composition; at the age of eighteen he married a girl eight years older than himself, Anne Hathaway, who gave him a child the following year and twins in 1585. Little else is known of his early life, and so we cannot tell what made him decide to leave Stratford in 1586 for London, where he stayed until 1611. In London he must soon have attracted attention because by 1592 he was popular enough a writer and actor to be sneered at by an older dramatist and university man as an uneducated jack-of-all-trades. He is mentioned as being among the principal actors of the city as early as 1598, and in 1599 we find that he is a member of the company running the Globe Theatre, with one-tenth interest in the profits – showing a business sense rarely seen in his fellow writers. His popularity is indicated by the fact that not only were his own plays published under his name (a rare procedure in his day) but also plays by others are to be found attributed to him, as if to indicate that his name alone would guarantee a good sale. An anthology of contemporary literature published in 1598 lists all of his plays (up to that date) and places him at the head of his contemporaries. Shakespeare must have been careful with his money; he bought up property in his home town, including the second biggest house in Stratford, where in 1611, again for no known reason, he retired to live the life of a rich country gentleman till his death in 1616.

Shakespeare's genius With Shakespeare, more perhaps than with any other writer, our ignorance of his life and opinions matters very little; in his plays we need make no allowances for him, but are presented with an almost godlike insight into a number of different types of person, and can only wonder how one man can have known so much about so many, and have shown it without the least revelation of his personality. It is best to forget our ignorance of his character and of much of his life and instead to concentrate on his works. These may conveniently be divided into five more or less chronological groups.

1. Apprenticeship 1586–1593 It is difficult to establish a firm date for Shakespeare's early plays; the evidence is scanty and often conflicting and in any case it is possible – or even probable – that he wrote only parts of the earliest plays which are usually included in his collected works. One of the most popular types of drama at the end of the sixteenth century was the chronicle play, a sort of 'real life' drama written around events which were still alive, if not exactly fresh, in the minds of people who went to see plays. The Wars of the Roses, for example, had been over for more than a century, but histories and stories and ballads had kept them in the public memory, just as in our own day the public interest in the events and incidents of the First World War seems to be as keen as it was some sixty years ago. It is not surprising, therefore, that playwrights and theatre managers, looking round for subjects to attract the public, turned to these wars which had torn England apart so tragically in the previous century. Shakespeare had read some at least of the history books, but he knew that in any case his audience would be familiar with the main 'stories' and the principal characters.

The first play in which his hand is clearly recognizable is *Henry VI, Part I*. (Some critics believe that it is nearly all Shakespeare's handiwork; others that he wrote only parts of it.) It was probably written in 1589–1590 and produced in 1591. The Second and Third Parts of *Henry VI* followed in quick succession. Other early plays include *Love's Labour's Lost* (c. 1594) – a rich and elegant comedy which is apparently wholly Shakespeare's – two comedies [*A Comedy of Errors* (about 1591) and *Two Gentlemen of Verona* (1591–1592)] based on Latin plays by Plautus and a gory tragedy, also based on Roman origins, *Titus Andronicus* (1593–1594), with some fine Shakespearean passages among the horrors. It was typical of the age, when the theatre was expanding rapidly but new and original plays were hard to come by, that as a change from chronicle plays the playwrights, of whom Shakespeare was only one, should turn to the Classics for ideas; after all, they had studied these works at school and university and the best plays and stories were already known to many in their audiences.

2. Growing success 1593–1599 It is unwise to think that Shakespeare divided his professional life into definite periods or that his works can similarly be placed in water-tight compartments. For example, *Richard III* and *King John* (both about 1593) belong chronologically, and partly in content, to his 'Apprenticeship' period yet both show many signs of growing maturity. But when, in 1594, he became one of 'The Lord Chamberlain's Men', the leading theatrical company of the day, his apprenticeship was surely finished and he was firmly set on the road to success. With colleagues like Richard Burbage, the great tragic actor, and Will Kempe, the most popular comic actor, he was among the top artists in their profession and was inspired to write at his most brilliant. (He was even happy to play small parts on the stage with them.) Comedies like *As You Like It* and *Twelfth Night*, histories like *Richard III*, *Henry IV* and *Henry V* and tragedies like *Romeo and Juliet* and *Julius Caesar* flowed from his brain and his pen in an astonishing succession. It was one of the most excitingly productive few years in the history of the theatre. It saw not only the production of some of the most popular plays, like *A Midsummer Night's Dream* and *The Merchant of Venice*, but the creation of some of the most famous (and best-loved) characters, from Bottom to Shylock, from Sir Toby Belch to Beatrice and Benedict, from Falstaff to King Henry V.

From this period, too, the boundaries between types of drama were becoming blurred. There is a growing awareness that, in the words of a later writer, life is a 'tangled skein'. There are hints of something approaching tragedy in comedies like *The Merchant of Venice* and *Much Ado About Nothing* and there is rich comedy in some of the Histories. Shakespeare's growing interest in his characters, and his deeper appreciation of the subtleties in human nature as a whole, are reflected in the general broadening of his ideas on what makes a successful and moving play. *Richard II* (1593), for example, could almost be a sketch for *Hamlet* (1602–1603) and the Antony of *Julius Caesar* (1599) foreshadows the Antony of *Antony and Cleopatra* (1607–1608).

3. The tragic phase 1599–1608 In 1599 Shakespeare's company acquired the famous Globe Theatre, the biggest public theatre in England at that time; in 1603, when Queen Elizabeth died, the Lord Chamberlain's Men became the King's Men under the generous patronage of James I, and were as successful at court as they were with the public. The plays of this period include the great tragedies, *Macbeth*, *Othello*, *King Lear* and *Hamlet*, the Roman plays, *Julius Caesar*, *Coriolanus* and *Antony and Cleopatra*, and what are sometimes called the 'problem plays', *Timon of Athens*, *Troilus and Cressida*, *All's Well that Ends Well* and *Measure for Measure*. In all of them we see ideas from earlier plays developed with a sureness and mastery which is phenomenal, with less emphasis on characterization (although the characters are still supremely well created and developed) and more on imagery and themes. The 'problem plays' are so called because, while drawing on the traditional schools of comedy, tragedy and history, they do not fall clearly into any of these categories. Shakespeare's vision of humanity, it has been said, was too far-ranging to be simple, and for these plays especially no generalization will suffice to explain the nature of that vision.

4. The last plays 1608–1611 In 1608 the King's Men bought a new theatre, the Blackfriars, which was more comfortable and expensive and, above all, indoors; although performances continued at the Globe until it was burnt down (traditionally on the first night of *Henry VIII*) the last plays seem to require the cosier and relatively luxurious atmosphere of the 'private' indoor theatre. Apart from *Henry VIII*, which was written in collaboration with another playwright, the last four plays, *Pericles*, *Cymbeline*, *The Winter's Tale* and *The Tempest*, form a remarkable unity and a fitting close to the dramatist's career. In all of them bold use is made of devices which in a lesser writer would seem farcical, and many critics have found that the demands they make on the reader's credulity and imagination are excessive. But it is well to remind ourselves that they were not written to be read and the skill of Shakespeare can inspire that 'willing suspension of disbelief' in things seen on the stage which the reader finds it more difficult to achieve. In any case, these four plays present a vision of beauty and harmony, in which suffering gives way to forgiveness, and misfortune to joy and reconciliation, presented in a form of poetical drama which, for all its subtlety, is an expression of the direct and simple truths of human affections and their magic.

From then till now For over two centuries after his death, Shakespeare's genius was admired by the critics and neglected by the theatre, which was happy to rewrite, to 'improve' and 'polish' his plays into something more closely resembling contemporary theatre. In our own century we have seen a reaction against this state of affairs, with a resurgence of interest in his plays *as* plays, and with striking and original attempts to bring together the discoveries of scholarship and the experience of the theatre-goer.

5. Shakespeare's poetry Even in his least 'great' plays Shakespeare showed that in his command of the language, his verbal inventiveness and imagery, his natural instinctive power to 'charm' the listener, he was perhaps above all else a poet. It was, in fact, as a poet that he set out – or almost. In 1593 he published his long poem *Venus and Adonis*, and in his Preface, addressed to the Earl of Southampton, he described it as 'the first heir of my invention'. This does not necessarily mean that it was his first written work; plays written to be performed were in a different class from books written to be read; in any case much of his work for the theatre hitherto had been editing, adaptation and a kind of 'writing to order' rather than sheer invention. In 1594 another long poem appeared, *The Rape of Lucrece*, also dedicated to the Earl of Southampton. That these poems were widely read and enjoyed (more, probably, than they are today) is shown by the fact that in Shakespeare's lifetime, seven editions of the first were issued and five of the second.

Some years later, in 1609, were published his *Sonnets*, and there is some reason to think that they were published without his permission. They were strictly personal poems but scholars all over the world have never established beyond a doubt either the identity of the people obscurely referred to in many of them or the person or persons to whom they were addressed. They vary in poetic quality but the finest of them reveal the same wisdom, the same depth of thought and the same supreme command of language that we find in the finest of his dramatic writing.

Finally we cannot ignore Shakespeare as a lyric poet. He lived in an age when people from every walk of life *sang* and his many songs reflect the passion for poetical words set to beautiful melodies, sad, sentimental, happy or merely narrative. Even Milton, a genius of a very different cast of mind, wrote affectionately, some fifteen or sixteen years after Shakespeare's death, of 'sweetest Shakespeare, Fancy's child' warbling 'his native wood-notes wild'.

II Suggestions on reading Shakespeare

When studying Shakespeare it is vital to remember that his plays were originally written not to be read but to be performed, that they contain a great deal of poetry, and that, because they were written more than 350 years ago, they contain some allusions with which we are not familiar and some words which we no longer use. Apart from these difficulties, they may be read as any other play; for the story, the characters, and the ideas about life which they present.

Dramatic reconstruction It is the job of the director, the producer and the actors to reconstruct the printed play, the words on the page, into the performance on the stage. Where no such stage performance is available the student or the reader must do this reconstruction for himself (or herself) *in the imagination*. It becomes more necessary, in fact, to imagine the dialogue being spoken, the reactions of any other characters present, even the scenery and properties (if any). We do this, subconsciously of course, when we are reading a novel; but a novel is written to be read and the writer has usually done his best to help the imagination. With a play, a more conscious effort is required and it is not easy to sustain; but it is worth the effort and luckily, since Shakespeare wrote for a theatre using little or no scenery, he himself often 'writes in' the background in words spoken by his characters. This technique – which the reader comes to apply almost without effort in time – not only goes a long way to familiarizing the reader with the details of the action; it also enables him to 'get inside' the characters themselves and to understand their motives and personalities.

Rereading and memorizing It is impossible to lay down any rule in this matter. Some students will want to reread some scenes over and over again, partly because they feel that such scenes cannot be fully grasped without many rereadings, partly because they enjoy certain scenes more than others. The same is true about memorizing; some speeches seem to cry out to be learnt by heart; they are dramatically and poetically superb pieces of writing and add to the possessions of a richly filled mind. Other students are less impressed by the 'set pieces'; they prefer to memorize a few short speeches, even single lines – although these often stay in the memory without being purposely memorized.

One thing, however, is certain. It is advisable – even compulsory – to read straight through a Shakespeare play once! Such a rapid reading will leave many points unclear, many words and phrases unexplained; but it will give the reader the elements of the story. A second reading will give opportunities to get a firmer hold of the structure of the play, the details of the plot, the importance of the various characters. All will now be ready for the *detailed* study – the imagery, the variations of tone, the personalities involved, the allusions and the difficult words and phrases.

Character analysis While Shakespeare took his plots ready-made from other authors, usually altering them only slightly, his genius shows in the way in which he creates characters which appear completely convincing as individuals. Although they act in what must obviously be a fore-ordained manner, they give the impression that their activities are absolutely spontaneous, indeed inevitable from such a character.

We shall see how the characters reveal their natures through what they do, what they say and how they say it, though their relationships with other people and sometimes through similarity to or contrast with them, and through what other people say about them or how they act concerning them. In these ways Shakespeare creates characters of a depth and complexity unsurpassed by any other dramatist. Nevertheless we must always remember that the characters are alive only in the bounds of the play. Much of their lives and personalities is perforce left out of consideration and we must not invent for them characteristics of which Shakespeare tells us nothing. Sometimes extra information can be gleaned from the source, but even this should be treated warily, since Shakespeare would alter or omit details to suit his own conception of the character or the theme of the play.

III General introduction to the play

Date of publication. The chronology of Shakespeare's plays is far from certain, but the consensus of opinion of leading modern scholars is that *King Henry IV, Part II* was written about 1597 and published in 1600.

Sources. For the serious matter of both parts, Shakespeare went to Holinshed's *Chronicles* (1587 Edition), and possibly for some material to Hall's *The Union of the two noble and illustre famelics of Lancaster and Yorke* (1550), Elyot's *Governour*, Stow's *Chronicles* and Daniel's *Civil Wars*. For his comic plot, Shakespeare probably found suggestions in the slight Chronicle play, *The Famous Victories of Henry V* (1588), or possibly Shakespeare drew upon a still older play upon which that crude chronicle play might have been based.

Style. Through the complementary actions and characters of Falstaff and Prince Henry, Shakespeare attempts to gain a dramatic unity of the serious and the comic in the play, but this unity is lessened considerably in *Part II* by the Prince's repudiation of his erstwhile companion. About half the scenes in this part are devoted to Falstaff, and through this comic element Prince Hal's not too admirable nature is expressed. The plot is slight and no central action predominates; the play is slow-moving, and there are many structural weaknesses.

The players. Although more detailed remarks on the main characters appear in subsequent sections of these Notes, it is essential, at the outset, for the student to become familiar with the various players and their names; thus they may be briefly introduced as follows:

Rumour, 'painted full of tongues', an allegorical figure, who appears first to give the audience the link between this play and *Henry IV, Part I.*

King Henry IV, who continues to suffer from a guilty conscience.

Henry, Prince of Wales, afterwards King Henry V, the madcap son of King Henry IV; in this play 'consideration like an angel, came and whipp'd the offending Adam out of him.'

Prince John of Lancaster, son of Henry IV and general of his father's forces, who breaks faith with the rebels in a most unjust and dishonourable manner; foil to Prince Hal.

Other sons of Henry IV: Prince Humphrey of Gloucester, and Thomas, Duke of Clarence.

Counsellors of the King: the Earl of Warwick; the Earl of Surrey.

The Earl of Westmoreland: leader of the royal forces against the rebels.

Officers in the Royal Army: Gower; Harcourt; Blunt.

Leaders of the rebellion in the north: The Earl of Northumberland. Scroop, Archbishop of York; Lord Mowbray; Lord Hastings; Lord Bardolph; Sir John Coleville.

Retainers of Northumberland: Travers and Morton.

Lady Northumberland: wife of the Earl and mother of the dead Hotspur.

Lady Percy: widow of Hotspur.

The Lord Chief Justice of the King's Bench: the learned and intrepid judge who was appointed by Henry V to continue to bear his 'unstained sword' of righteousness. 'Though not clean past (his) youth, (he) hath yet some smack of age in (him), some relish of the saltness of time.'

A servant of the Lord Chief Justice.

Sir John Falstaff, 'a fool and a jester', who requires 'two and twenty yards of satin' for a suit. To Prince Hal he is the nimble-witted and irresponsible companion, who follows 'the young Prince up and down like his ill angel'; to King Henry V 'the tutor and feeder of (the) riots of (his) youth' – foil to the Lord Chief Justice.

Falstaff's page, 'a little tiny thief', 'fitter to be worn in (his) cap than to wait at (his) heels'.

Bardolph, Falstaff's drinking companion and corporal, an 'arrant malmsey-nose knave'.

Peto, another of Falstaff's companions.

Pistol, Falstaff's ensign, a ranting 'swaggerer', a 'mouldy rogue', whose bombastic words quoted from scraps of blood-curdling plays conceal a cowardly heart.

Poins, Prince Hal's companion at the Boar's Head Tavern.

Mistress Quickly, hostess of the Boar's Head Tavern in Eastcheap, whose reputation for respectability constantly threatens to break down.

Doll Tearsheet, a prostitute at the Boar's Head Tavern with a vitriolic vocabulary.

Fang and **Snare,** sheriff's officers who prove no match for Falstaff.

Robert Shallow, 'a poor esquire ... and one of the King's justices of the peace', conceited victim of Falstaff's capacity for borrowing.

Silence, another country justice, friend and admirer of Shallow.

Davy, Shallow's servant.

Falstaff's unpromising recruits for the Royal Army: Ralph Mouldy ('young, strong, and of good friends'); Simon Shadow (a 'half-faced fellow'); Thomas Wart ('a very ragged wart'); Francis Feeble (a woman's tailor, 'as valiant as the wrathful dove'); Peter Bullcalf (a 'diseased man').

First Beadle, a 'damn'd trip-visag'd rascal', a 'blue-bottle rogue'.

Other characters: Lords and Attendants, a Porter, Beadles, Grooms, etc., a Dancer who speaks the Epilogue.

IV The historical background

The scene of the whole action is England in the early part of the fifteenth century (1403–1413).

The rule of the three Edwards. For a correct understanding of the political situation in England at the time of Henry IV, it is necessary to go back as far as the reign of *Edward I* (1272–1307). Edward I was one of the greatest of England's kings and during the thirty-five years of his reign much progress in the right direction was made in his country. Apart from his conquest of Wales, the King did much to shape the form of English government of the future through his 'Model Parliament' of 1295 which included representatives from the commoners instead of only the lords and the higher clergy – although it must also be said that this reform was granted by the King because he was in need of money, a need which arose from his wars against Scotland and France.

Edward I was followed, however, by a weak ruler in *Edward II* (1307–1327), who married Isabella of France. Unfortunately, Edward ruled his country very largely through favourites whom he selected from among those around him; one of these, Piers Gaveston – the King's foster-brother – was a much hated figure, and in 1310 the barons forced the King to surrender power into the hands of the 'Lords Ordainers'; Gaveston was beheaded. On the field of battle, Edward II was no more successful, and his attempt to continue his father's campaign against the Scots led to the defeat of the English forces at Bannockburn in 1314.

After Gaveston's death, the King's new favourites were the two Despensers, father and son, but they were in 1321 banished by Parliament. In reply Edward took up arms against the barons, captured the Earl of Lancaster (whom he beheaded) and recalled the Despensers – now the virtual rulers of England. The Lords Ordainers now saw the hopelessness of their trying to take power from the King without the help of the commons, and therefore the barons, along with the commons, called a Parliament in 1327 and declared Edward II unfit to rule. The King resigned in favour of his son. Queen Isabella had given quite considerable help to the lords in securing the overthrow of her husband, for she was jealous of the favourites whom her husband had gathered around him. Edward was later brutally murdered by Roger Mortimer.

The next king was *Edward III* (1327–1377). He cannot be said to have ruled his country, however, until the overthrow of Isabella and Mortimer in 1330. During the reign of Edward III, there broke out (in 1338) the 'Hundred Years' War' with France, although there were intervening years of peace. Edward laid claim to the French throne, and from 1340 took the title of 'King of France'. Although meeting with initial victories, by 1375 the only land held by the English in France was Calais, which remained in England's hands until 1558.

The later years of Edward III saw internal difficulties; for the King had sunk into his dotage; his eldest son, Edward the Black Prince (heir to the throne), was in ill health, and died in 1376; and it was thought that Edward's fourth son, John of Gaunt, Duke of Lancaster (who had married Blanche, heiress of Henry of Lancaster) would seek to gain succession to the throne.

From Richard II to Henry IV. When Edward III died in 1377, however, 'the fear that John of Gaunt, Duke of Lancaster, would seize the throne proved to be unfounded. Lancaster was true to the knightly ideals of his age and, notwithstanding his arrogance, did not aim at usurpation' (Williams and Walker, *History of England*, p. 153). The new King was Richard II (1377–1399), son of the Black Prince. Richard ascended the throne at the age of ten. Although John of Gaunt proved loyal to the Crown (Lancaster retired to his estates, although some of his followers were dismissed from office), yet trouble faced the reign of Richard through the teachings of John Wycliffe, who launched his attack against the established Church and who had, without doubt, much to do with the outbreak of the 'Peasants' Revolt' (1381).

Richard's youth on his accession to the throne naturally meant that in the early years of his reign much of the power was in the hands of his ministers. Two prominent advisers to Richard were the Earl of Suffolk and the Earl of Oxford (created by Richard Duke of Ireland). The government of the country was a failure, however, and thus the Duke of Gloucester, the King's youngest uncle, raise a party to oppose the Crown. He was joined by Henry of Bolingbroke (son of John of Gaunt and later Henry IV), and the Earls of Nottingham, Warwick and Arundel; with the other nobles who supported them, they came to be known as the Lords Appellant. In 1388, the Lords Appellant succeeded in having Suffolk and Oxford and the other courtiers who supported Richard condemned as traitors; Oxford and Suffolk, however, managed to escape to live a life of exile.

In 1389, Richard resumed the government of his country, telling Gloucester and his friends that he was now old enough to manage his own affairs; the King was, however wise enough not to attempt to recall his exiled ministers. Indeed, he kept many of the Lords Appellant in his Council, and when John of Gaunt returned from Spain in 1389 Richard even looked to him for advice. For a while, peace and prudent rule were the order of things; hostilities against France, too, were temporarily ended, and Richard took the daughter of Charles VI of France as his second wife.

In spite of the happier conditions of rule, however, the King never forgave the Lords Appellant. Henry of Bolingbroke and the Earl of Nottingham had come over to the side of the King, but in 1397 the other Lords Appellant were either beheaded or banished by the revengeful Richard. Bolingbroke and Nottingham, in return for their support, were given the Dukedoms of Hereford and Norfolk respectively. Bolingbroke and Nottingham quarrelled, however, and Richard seized this opportunity (in 1398) to banish both of them.

While Henry Bolingbroke was in exile, his father, John of Gaunt, Duke of Lancaster, died, and Richard II seized his vast estate. In July, 1399, therefore, Henry Bolingbroke, in company with Arundel, Archbishop of Canterbury, landed at Ravenspur (Ravenspurgh in the text of *Henry IV, Part I*) to claim from Richard the Duchy of Lancaster.

On landing in England, Henry Bolingbroke secured the support of Henry Percy, Earl of Northumberland, and others. Henry then decided to claim the throne of England. The King was absent in Ireland, whither he had gone in an endeavour to restore peace, and when he arrived back in England he found that the whole country had deserted him, and thus Richard had no other course than to submit. The King's abdication was approved by Parliament, which also passed a statute settling the Crown on Henry IV (Bolingbroke) and his heirs. The genealogical table shows that Henry IV was the son of John of Gaunt, Duke of Lancaster, *fourth* son of Edward III, while the nearest heir by blood was Edmund Mortimer, Earl of March, who claimed his right to succeed through Lionel, Duke of Clarence, *third* son of Edward III.

Henry IV was the first of the Lancastrian kings. Under this dynasty the former toleration gave way to a system of persecution of all forms of heresy and to a rigid insistance on orthodoxy in religion and constitutional government in secular affairs. Men of learning were quickly frightened away from Lollardy and the movement declined. On the other hand, as H. A. L. Fisher observes in his *History of Europe*, Parliament took full advantage of the new dynasty to obtain control of legislation and finance. And, although this constitutional advance was not maintained during the fifteenth century, it was the precedent first established by the Lancastrian Parliaments which inspired common lawyers in the great struggle between the crown and Parliament in the seventeenth century.

History of the early rebellion. King Henry IV bestowed considerable gifts and honours on the Duke of Northumberland in an endeavour to retain his loyalty, and indeed at first his family, the Percys, served the King with distinction. Henry Percy (Hotspur) the son of the Duke of Northumberland took part in the campaign against the Welsh and in 1402 defeated a Scottish army at the Battle of Homilon Hill. But shortly afterwards the Percys defected and joined the Welsh leader Owen Glendower.

The Welsh revolt began as a result of a dispute over land rights between Owen Glendower and his English neighbour Lord Gray of Ruthin. Glendower felt himself unjustly treated by the House of Lords in adjudicating on the matter and raised an army to assert his rights. This private feud escalated into a national rebellion in which the Welsh people rallied round Glendower to assert their national independence.

At first Glendower was successful and Henry IV's attempts to put down his rebellion were hampered by lack of money. His troops moreover were at a disadvantage in the mountainous terrain of North Wales where the first clashes between the rebels and the King's men took place. Very soon Glendower had complete control of the north and was extending his power into the southern part of Wales.

When the Percys joined forces with Glendower in the summer of 1403 the rebellion had reached its most ominous stage and Henry's

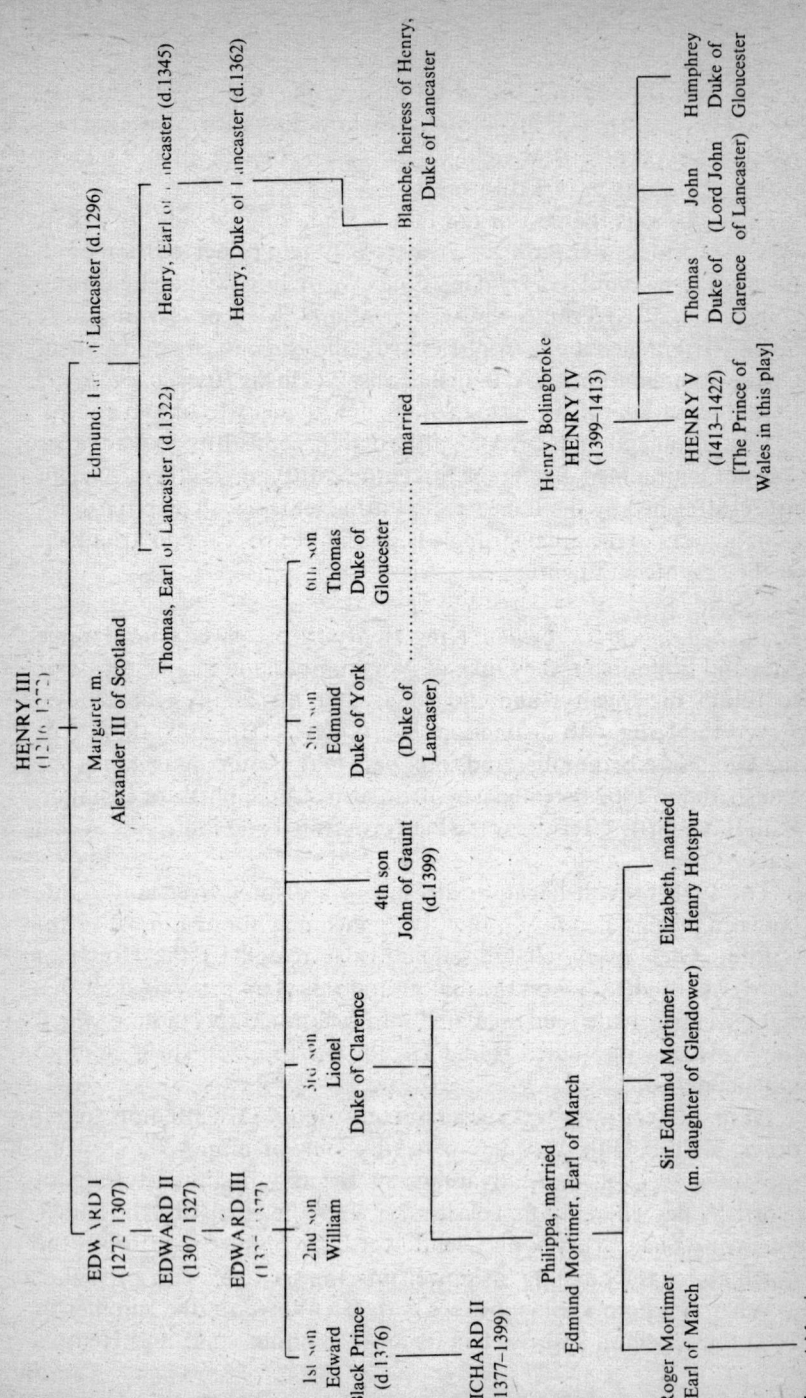

position as monarch was in jeopardy. At the Battle of Shrewsbury however the King defeated the combined forces brought together by Hotspur and Douglas both of whom were killed. The critical phase of the rebellion was passed.

The latter part of Henry IV's rule. Even after the Battle of Shrewsbury the danger to Henry IV's throne was not yet over. The north was still in a state of ferment, the war in Wales went on, and a French fleet ravaged the southern coast with impunity. Henry's vigilance and activity were, however, equal to the task. A fresh outbreak of rebellion in the north was crushed at Shipton Moor in 1405. Scroop, Archbishop of York, and Mowbray, Earl Marshal, who led the rebels, were taken and executed. Thereafter, a final rebellion was put down in the north, and Glendower was driven back into his mountains (1408).

All these crises had, however, compelled Henry IV to make important concessions to the House of Commons: throughout his reign he was hampered by want of money, and the regular exercise by Parliament of the right to withhold supplies gave that body great control over his actions. Thus limited, his foreign policy was not energetic, and, although he seized the opportunity afforded by civil war to invade France (1411), his efforts were in general confined to strengthening his dynasty by foreign marriages.

Meanwhile, his eldest son, Prince Henry, having driven Glendower back to Snowdon, rapidly gained experience in administrative affairs, until, by 1410, he was head of the Royal Council. The stories of the Prince's youthful extravagances and dissoluteness are highly improbable, and, though his father appears to have been jealous of his popularity, he was practically at the head of affairs for some years before the death of Henry IV.

In his later years Henry IV was a confirmed invalid, and had to entrust more and more power to his eldest son, with whom he was not always on the best of terms. He died on 20 March 1413, and was buried at Canterbury. Three weeks later (9 April) Prince Henry was crowned Henry V, and entered upon his inheritance with the goodwill of all classes of the nation. So unanimous was the support he met with in Parliament that constitutional affairs ceased to have any interest during his reign. The great objective of his policy was the conquest of France, and it was with this aim in view that he issued a general amnesty on his succession, and appealed to the nation as a whole to support him.

V Brief outline of the plot

Since the theme of *Henry IV, Part II* is frequently complicated and there is a bewildering list of characters, it is essential for the student to possess some knowledge of the general sweep of the action before any attempt can be made to summarize the play scene by scene. The brief outline of the plot given below should be consulted more frequently while reading the play and the complete summary which follows.

Act one
Despite early rumours that Hotspur has defeated the royalist forces and slain the Crown Prince, the true report of the defeat of the insurgents and the death of the impetuous young leader is finally brought to the Earl of Northumberland together with the news that Prince John of Lancaster and the Earl of Westmoreland are leading an army against him. The enraged earl plans to join forces with the Archbishop of York in meeting the royal army. In London, Sir John Falstaff is finding it difficult to bid farewell to his associates of the Boer's Head Tavern and to start north with the King's commission to enlist en route soldiers for the army that is advancing against the rebels.

Act two
Falstaff's 'hasty employment in the King's affairs' helps to save him from being arrested for debt at the suit of Mistress Quickly, the hostess of the Tavern, and the clever old rascal concludes the whole matter by borrowing still more money from her and rioting and jesting with Prince Hal and other companions until messengers from the King summon both merry-makers to their army duties against the rebels. In the North, the Earl of Northumberland's wife and daughter-in-law, Hotspur's widow, prevail upon the cold-blooded nobleman to desert the Archbishop of York and take refuge in Scotland until a more fitting opportunity arises for rebellion.

Act three
In Westminster Palace the King, enfeebled by anxieties and ill-health, discusses the rebellion with his counsellors, the Earl of Warwick and the Earl of Surrey. As the monarch beholds the truth of Richard II's prophecy regarding Northumberland, he realizes that 'uneasy lies the head that wears a crown' and wishes that 'these inward wars (were) once out of hand' so that he might make his long-deferred expedition to Jerusalem. While the sick King courts sleep to 'steep (his) senses in forgetfulness', the irresponsible Falstaff is in Gloucestershire at the house of Justice Shallow, where he misuses 'the King's press damnably' by allowing likely recruits for the northern army to buy themselves off while he enlists only a crew of ragged scarecrows.

Act four
In the insurgent camp in Yorkshire, the rebel Archbishop of York with Mowbray (son of Bolingbroke's old enemy), Hastings, and others are chilled by the news of the Earl of Northumberland's defection. Through the agency of the Earl of Westmoreland the rebel leaders are prevailed upon to present a schedule of their various grievances to John of Lancaster and these the Prince swears 'by the honour of (his) blood' to redress with speed. Upon this 'princely word' the rebel armies are dispersed; but no sooner have the insurgents disbanded than the perjured Prince orders the rebel noblemen to be executed, and their miserable followers to be pursued and slaughtered. The report of this treacherous act reaches the King in Westminster together with the news that Northumberland and Lord Bardolph have been defeated by the Sheriff of Yorkshire. But the King is too sick to hear even good tidings; putting his crown upon his pillow, he falls into a coma, and the Crown Prince, summoned to the palace and alone in the chamber with his father, thinks the King is dead and sorrowfully removes from the room the golden circlet of his father's cares. Awakening alone and misunderstanding his son's action, the King accuses him of desiring his death, but the genuine grief of the young Prince then becomes apparent, and the two are reconciled. The dying monarch advises his son to 'busy giddy minds with foreign quarrels' so that the rebellion at home may slumber. He is then carried off to die in the 'Jerusalem Chamber', thus fulfilling a prophecy that he 'should not die but in Jerusalem'.

Act five
Upon the death of his father, Prince Hal becomes ruler as Henry V. The news of these events speeds to Gloucestershire, and Falstaff hurries to London to reap the benefits of his long companionship with the Prince. But he finds that the young King is not the riotous boon companion of old. The new monarch rebukes him publicly and orders his arrest and banishment at the hands of the Lord Chief Justice. Thus having made a public demonstration of high purposes, Henry V plans to assemble Parliament to discuss an invasion of France.

VI Summary of the play

Induction
In this prologue-scene *Rumour* is personified, 'painted full of tongues'. Arriving before Warkworth Castle, home of Northumberland (the nominal leader of the rebels against Henry IV) she announces the victory of the King's forces at Shrewsbury. Then, abruptly, remembering her true character, she spreads false reports so that the 'crafty-sick' Northumberland may believe that the rebels under Hotspur (Northumberland's son) may have been victorious.

Act one
Scene one. A Porter appears on the wall above the gate at the entry of Warkworth Castle to admit *Lord Bardolph* (one of the leaders of the rebellion in the North). The *Earl of Northumberland*, hobbling upon a crutch and with his head muffled, then comes out of the orchard and eagerly demands to hear Bardolph's tidings. The latter declares that at Shrewsbury the rebel party has gained a great victory: the King himself has been badly wounded, Prince Harry has been 'slain outright', many important prisoners have been taken, while the rest of the royal army is in flight. But the Earl displays great caution in accepting this report, and is busily cross-examining Bardolph when *Travers* (one of the Earl's retainers) arrives with different tidings: he has heard that the rebellion has 'had bad luck' and that Hotspur himself has been slain. The disabused Earl resists reassuring arguments from Bardolph, and the party awaits the approach of *Morton* (another of Northumberland's retainers). The Earl instantly recognizes in Morton's face, before the servant has a chance to speak, the tragic confirmation of his worst fears.

Morton describes the disastrous battle at Shrewsbury, telling how the 'never-daunted' Hotspur was killed by Prince Henry, how the rebel Earls of Douglas and Worcester were taken prisoners, and how many of the other rebel leaders deserted before the onslaught of the victorious royal forces. Mortimer concludes his gloomy tidings by stating that Lancaster and Westmoreland are now leading forces against the remnants of the rebels, including Northumberland himself.

The Earl staggers under the blow of the final knowledge of his son's death, and then, striving to throw off his sickness, he suddenly displays a martial energy and speaks of donning his armour to avenge Hotspur. But this sudden outburst, far from impressing his hearers with his warlike spirit, alarms them for his health, and Morton prevails upon him to 'divorce not wisdom from your honour'. He points out that the earl was well aware beforehand that his son would be in the thick of danger, yet he was not in a position to restrain Hotspur from giving battle. Bardolph then takes up where Morton has left off: now that they have lost the first round and brave Hotspur has been killed, it is necessary for them, under Northumberland's guidance, to make fresh plans and to gather new strength.

Morton then tries to hearten his master further by relating how the 'gentle Archbishop of York' has promised to support the rebels; he points out that Hotspur's followers, unnerved by being aware that they were rebels, were not able to give a good account of themselves against the King's forces; but now the Archbishop, by leading his office and character, sanctifies rebellion, so that the insurgents will be able to fight with restored confidence in their cause.

The Earl of Northumberland, encouraged by these tidings, thereupon asks the three men to join him within, where they can hold a meeting to devise the best ways of gathering their scattered supporters together.

Scene two. In a London street, *Sir John Falstaff*, hobbling with a stick, and followed by his diminutive *page* bearing his sword, is in ill humour. He contrasts the mandrake-like appearance of his page with his own huge bulk, and declares that he feels 'like a sow that hath overwhelmed all her litter but one'; he is convinced that his comrade, the Prince, has provided this minute attendant 'to set him off'. Falstaff is also annoyed with his mercer, Master Dombledon, who has refused to furnish him with a new satin outfit until better security can be provided.

As he is busy denouncing Dombledon as a rascally glutton, Falstaff perceives the *Lord Chief Justice* approaching, accompanied by a servant. As the Chief Justice had recently received a box on the ear from the prince, Falstaff's boon companion, and as warrants from the Sheriff have been out for Falstaff himself concerning an alleged robbery, the latter has no wish to encounter this representative of the law, and quickly turns down a side alley, followed by his page. Thereupon the Chief Justice sends his servant to recall Sir John, who feigns deafness. This subterfuge is soon dismissed by the Chief Justice himself, who obviously still resents Falstaff's earlier offence. Falstaff artfully proceeds to turn the conversation upon the king's indisposition, a topic which the Chief Justice cannot lightly brush aside without discourtesy. At the same time, his anger is blunted by hearing from his servant a good report of Falstaff's actions at Shrewsbury. Nevertheless he proceeds to admonish Falstaff for his evil influence on the young Prince; in fact, declares the Chief Justice, Falstaff is like an 'ill angel' to the prince. He continues by declaring that, although Falstaff behaves like a young blade, yet his skin is withered, his beard is white, and he shows many other signs of approaching dotage. Falstaff's resources are put to the severest test in the encounter of wits that follows. But, quite unabashed by the Lord Chief Justice's strong attack on his character, Falstaff concludes the interview by asking the judge to lend him a thousand pounds 'to furnish him forth' for his expedition to the north with Lord John of Lancaster against the Archbishop and the Earl of Northumberland.

This request sends the Chief Justice hurrying on his way, and Falstaff, after learning from his page that he has only seven goats and twopence left in his purse, reflects on the 'incurable disease' of poverty which constantly haunts his footsteps. He thereupon despatches letters about the forthcoming expedition to the Prince, Lancaster and Westmoreland, and sends his page off with a fourth letter to Mrs Ursula, whom he has sworn to marry, asking her for a loan.

Scene three. The scene now changes to the palace of Scroop, the *Archbishop of York*, who is holding a conference with the rebel leaders *Hastings*, *Mowbray* and Lord Bardolph, who has ridden from Warkworth. They are relying on Northumberland for active support and for supplies, but Bardolph warns them not to expect any assistance from that quarter in estimating their ability to oppose the King. But Hastings urges that the King has to divide his forces to be able to meet attacks from the Welsh and the French, so that he will not be able to spare sufficent troops to counter their rebellion in the north.

The Archbishop points out that both the King's plans and their own support from the people are not assured, and he is particularly fearful of the commons, which was fickle when it applauded Bolingbroke, fickle when it would have Richard die, and fickle when it would have him live again. Thus, although they must profess to support the will of the people, the Archbishop indicates that he really has little faith in the cause of the rebellion. Nevertheless, the Archbishop has made up his mind to join the insurgents and gives orders for immediate action.

Act two

Scene one. Near the Boar's Head Tavern at Eastcheap (south-east London), *Mistress Quickly*, the Tavern's hostess, is speaking to *Sergeant Fang* and *Yeoman Snare* (the former a large villainous fellow, the latter thin and undersized) about the action for debt which she has brought against Falstaff. She tells them how Falstaff has continually borrowed from her in the past, until he now owes her one hundred marks, which he has made no effort to repay, despite repeated promises. She speaks of herself as 'a poor lone woman', and urges them not to fail in their duty of arresting him. From their replies, however, it is apparent that neither Fang nor Snare relish coming to grips with Falstaff, who is a deft swordsman.

At that moment Falstaff, his page and *Bardolph*, an 'arrant malmsey-nose knave', come along the street; Fang attempts to arrest Sir John 'at the suit of Mistress Quickly', but a scuffle ensues, in which Bardolph, the page, and hostess take part; yet the sheriff's men gain the upper hand, with assistance from members of the crowd which has meanwhile been attracted to the spot, and Falstaff is on the point of being arrested when the Lord Chief Justice and his men arrive.

Thereupon Mistress Quickly scolds Falstaff as a 'honey-seed, a man-queller', and with much circumlocution tries to state her case to the Lord Chief Justice; yet, at the same time, she laments losing such a profitable customer as well as a prospective husband, declaring that Falstaff has promised to marry her. Sir John slyly intervenes to remark to the Chief Justice that 'she says up and down the town that her eldest son is like you'. But the judge, after further inquiry, bids Falstaff 'satisfy the poor woman'; thereupon Sir John draws her aside, cajoling her into withdrawing the action, and, in fact, wheedles the hostess into making a further loan, which she can only raise by pawning her plate and tapestry.

Meanwhile, *Gower*, one of the officers in the Royal Army, has arrived on the scene to bring tidings to the Chief Justice from the king. He reports that Henry IV is near at hand, having slept the previous night at Basingstoke, while two thousand of the royal forces, under the lead of Prince John, have gone north as a vanguard against Northumberland's rebels.

Mistress Quickly, confusedly satisfied, goes off with Bardolph, the officers and the page, while Falstaff, now free of the fear of arrest and filled with his own importance about his forthcoming military service, asks 'Master Gower' to dine or sup with him, and seizes the opportunity of a final gibe at the Lord Chief Justice, incurring, however, only a contemptuous dismissal to which even Falstaff has no reply.

Scene two. *Prince Henry* and his companion, *Poins*, both recently arrived from Wales, enter a room in the Prince's house in London. Flinging himself down on a couch, the Prince speaks to Poins, with humorous bitterness, of a certain sense of disgrace in Poins's companionship; he vents his disgust upon Poins's dissipated habits, and states that his companion is always seeking entertainment for himself but cannot provide clothing for his many illegitimate children. Henry's disgust with his old manner of living is sharpened by the tidings of his father's illness, especially when he hears that Poins takes for granted that this news can only be a matter for joy to the heir of England's throne.

Bardolph and Falstaff's page then arrive to deliver a letter of farewell from the fat knight on his departure for the north. Falstaff's page makes witty remarks to the Prince at the expense of Bardolph, whose red face he compares to an alewife's red petticoat and the red window-frames of taverns of ill repute. The Prince then reads aloud Falstaff's letter, in which the knight is carried away with feelings of his own importance, and in which he warns the Prince against Poins who, he alleges, is scheming to marry off his sister to the Prince.

Poins takes this letter in good humour, and, on hearing that Falstaff will be dining at the Eastcheap Tavern with Mistress Quickly and Doll Tearsheet, they resolve to play a parting trick on Sir John. Anxious to see Falstaff in his true colours with these women, while they themselves are unseen, the Prince and Poins decide to disguise themselves as barmen, Bardolph and the page being bribed to secrecy. Yet the prince enters into the spirit of the jest with little real gusto and with an acute sense of degradation, since he feels that it is a low transformation from 'a prince to a prentice'.

Scene three. Back at Northumberland's castle at Warkworth, *Lady Northumberland* and her daughter-in-law, Lady Percy (wife of the recently slain Hotspur), are earnestly attempting to persuade the earl not to carry out his resolve to lead the renewed rebellion against the King. When the Earl's wife sees that her efforts are not meeting with success, she tells Northumberland to 'Do what you will, your wisdom be your guide', and he emphatically replies that he cannot back down now as his 'honour is at pawn'. Taking up the argument against his participation in the new rebellion, Lady Percy begs her father-in-law not to go 'to these wars', and reminds him that he refused aid when her 'heart's dear Harry' needed him most (at Shrewsbury); his failure to honour his obligations then had cost her husband's life; thus, she asks, why should he go to battle now when nothing of comparable value is at stake? She then proceeds to lament and eulogize her dead husband. The earl's resolve to take part in the rebellion is obviously not very deep, for he is finally persuaded by his wife and daughter-in-law to flee to Scotland.

Scene four. Two drawers are laying a table with wine and fruit in a private room at the Boar's Head Tavern in Eastcheap; from their conversation it becomes clear that Falstaff and Mistress Quickly are dining in another room in the Tavern, and that they will soon be adjourning to the present room to wine and to listen to some hired musicians.

Hostess Quickly and *Doll Tearsheet* enter from the room on the left and Falstaff, singing fragments of an old ballad, comes in from the right. Having drunk 'too much canaries' (wine), Doll wrangles with Falstaff, yet would be friends with him since he is 'going to the wars'. One of the drawers then annouces that *Ancient Pistol* (one of Falstaff's associates, a braggart with a fine command of bombastic language) is downstairs and is anxious to converse with his master. Neither of the women is anxious for his company: the hostess declares that she 'cannot abide swaggerers', and that, having already been summoned for keeping a noisy, disreputable house, she has no wish again to come into contact with the law for admitting such dishonest gamesters and ruffians as Pistol; Mistress Tearsheet has no hesitation about calling Falstaff's crony 'the foul-mouth'dst rogue in England'. Despite their protests, Pistol enters, accompanied by Bardolph and Falstaff's diminutive page. After the ensign has greeted his master, he is reviled by Doll Tearsheet; he replies to her insults in a bombastic fashion, quoting disjointed extracts from bloodcurdling plays. Then Pistol, very much the worse for liquor, snatches up his sword to cut Doll to pieces, and, a brawl ensuing, he is turned out by Falstaff and Bardolph. Sir John then sheathes his sword and returns, panting and blowing, to his seat, where he is lauded by Doll as a 'sweet little rogue' for ejecting Pistol.

The musicians then enter, followed by the Prince and Poins, both of whom are disguised as drawers. They watch Doll sit on Falstaff's knee and fondle him, and listen to them converse amicably about themselves, Falstaff venting his opinions about the Prince with complete frankness, ascribing to both the Prince and Poins a number of habits mostly childish or disreputable. Yet, when Falstaff summons the 'drawers' to provide more wine, he speedily detects their disguises; with mock gravity, the Prince demands that Falstaff defend his statements. Sir John replies that his remarks were made in pure fun, that he meant no abuse, and that he is more firmly attached to the Prince than ever before.

These comic exchanges are abruptly interrupted by a loud knocking at the door. *Pet* (another of Falstaff's companions, but now 'an attendant on Prince Henry') is admitted with the news that the King is at Westminster and that there are grave tidings from the north. Feeling 'much to blame' for this turn of events, the Prince, accompanied by Poins, Peto and Bardolph, hastens away from the Tavern. Bardolph returns a moment later to inform Falstaff that the military authorities are anxious for his immediate services. As he leaves with Bardolph, Falstaff is bid a tearful farewell by Doll Tearsheet.

Act three
Scene one. It is past midnight in a room in the palace at Westminster: the King (Henry IV), outworn with sleeplessness, sends a page to summon Warwick and Surrey to counsel. The King then soliloquizes on sleep: he wonders how many humble folks in his kingdom 'are at this hour asleep', and is vexed that sleep chooses to visit smoky cottages rather than perfumed chambers; even the common ship-boy, high up on his mast out in the storm-tossed ocean, is lulled to sleep

by the waves' deafening roar, yet he, a king, is denied even partial sleep; 'uneasy lies the head that wears a crown', he reflects.

The King's two advisers, the earls of *Warwick* and *Surrey*, accompanied by Sir John *Blunt*, a high officer in the royal army, then arrive and bid the King 'good morrow'. The King reminds them that the news from the north is serious, the rebel forces outnumbering those sent to oppose them. Henry, speaking his thoughts aloud, wishes that man could look into the 'book of fate' and learn what the future holds in store for him. He reminds his advisers how, eight years before, Northumberland had deserted the cause of Richard II to support him (Henry). And recalls the words of Richard that 'the time shall come' when that act of treachery 'Shall break into corruption' and lead to the 'division of our amity'.

Warwick replies that there was nothing supernatural about Richard's prophecy and bids the King not to fear the Percys; rumour has exaggerated the size of the rebel army, so that the royal forces sent north will be fully capable of suppressing the rebellion. He further comforts the King with the news that Glendower, the Welsh rebel, is dead. Henry thereupon takes Warwick's advice to retire once more to bed, although he expresses the wish that these civil wars were finished, as he longs to go to the Holy Land.

Scene two. Two Gloucestershire justices, *Shallow* and *Silence*, meet each other before the former's house. While they await the arrival of Falstaff on his recruiting campaign, they discuss mutual family matters and bygone days, the garrulous Shallow boasting of his youthful exploits in London (when 'Jack Falstaff' was then 'a boy a page to Thomas Mowbray, Duke of Norfolk'), and lamenting the death of old acquaintances. Bardolph approaches and informs them of Falstaff's imminent arrival. They bicker over the word 'accommodated' which Bardolph has used in the sense of 'provided', a term which the justices do not understand.

Falstaff arrives and is warmly greeted by the two justices. With much agitation, Shallow then produces the roll of recruits:

Mouldy, 'a good-limbed fellow; young, strong, and of good friends' is the first to appear; he protests against his recruitment to Sir John, since he is his mother's only support.

Shadow, a gaunt man, is the next recruit, and Falstaff, aside, in a play upon the word 'shadow', hints at the practice of filling the recruiting book with bogus names for the drawing of extra pay.

Wart, the third recruit, is a tattered man, whom Falstaff at first rejects as a likely soldier.

Feeble, a timid little man and a woman's tailor, follows, and Falstaff, ironically declaring that 'courageous Feeble ... wilt be as valiant as the wrathful dove', includes him in the list of likely recruits.

Bullcalf, a stout young man, is also chosen despite his protestations that he suffers from a perpetual cough and cold!

Having pricked down the selected men, Shallow brags of old times at Clement's Inn, which, as Silence remarks, was 'fifty-five years ago'. The two justices then accompany Falstaff to have a drink.

During their absence, Bullcalf and Mouldy purchase their release from the army by bribing Bardolph, but Feeble refuses to stoop to such cowardice. Falstaff and the Justices then return, and Bardolph takes his master aside and informs him that 'I have three pound to free Mouldy and Bullcalf'. Thereupon, much to Justice Shallow's surprise, Falstaff decides to take as recruits only Wart (because of his ragged appearance), Shadow (because he presents no target to the enemy), and Feeble (because he will excel at retreating). The easily diverted Shallow thereupon takes up a musket to give a demonstration of how he once acted as 'Sir Dagonet' in a play in London. After inviting Falstaff to renew acquaintances on his return, Shallow, accompanied by the taciturn Silence, goes inside, while Bardolph marches off the recruits.

Left alone, Falstaff soliloquizes about Justice Shallow: he 'sees to the bottom' of the pompous squire's character; he remembers him as a youth in London, who had sung stale tunes to his mistresses, who had been as 'lecherous as a monkey', and who was always in the rear of fashion. Falstaff resolves that, on his return to Gloucestershire, he will secure a rich harvest of gold out of Shallow.

Act four
Scene one. The leaders of the northern rebellion (York, Bardolph, Mowbray, Hastings, and others), have met in Gaultree Forest, in Yorkshire, with their forces, expecting Northumberland's troops to join them there presently. The Archbishop, Scroop, states, however, that he has recently received letters from Northumberland announcing – with many good reasons and good wishes – his withdrawal to Scotland. A messenger comes up with the news that the King's forces are approaching, and are scarcely a mile off.

A moment later, *Westmoreland*, commander of the King's army, joins the rebel leaders with greetings from his master, Prince John of Lancaster. He takes the opportunity to reprove the Archbishop for having used his peaceful and religious office to lead men to war. In reply, the Archbishop relates to the envoy Westmoreland the grievances which have made him, a man of peace, take up arms: Scroop justifies the rebellion as having offered the best hope of removing the infection of the times and creating a peace in more than name. To Lord Mowbray, who would revive his father's wrongs, and who maintains that there can be no enduring peace with the King, Westmoreland answers that Mowbray has nothing 'to build an inch of grief on', and announces Prince John's willingness to hold a parley with the rebel leaders, since the latter's father (Henry IV) is weary of bickering. The envoy adds that should the rebels' grievances be found just then the Prince will redress them, although he warns them not to regard this offer as a sign of weakness, since the royal army is better equipped and is fighting for a better cause than they are.

The Archbishop agrees to such a meeting and places in Westmoreland's hands a schedule of grievances for the Prince to study, Westmoreland departs.

Alone once more, the rebel leaders listen to Mowbray voicing strong misgivings about the approaching conference; he is reassured by the Archbishop, who believes that the King, by no means popular among the people and gravely ill, will show them a politic clemency – an argument which is strongly supported by Hastings, who regards Henry IV as 'a fangless lion'.

Westmoreland returns to invite Scroop to meet the Prince midway between the armies.

Scene two. A few moments later *Prince John* himself appears, with Westmoreland, to negotiate the terms. To the Archbishop he speaks harshly as to one who has been the voice of God, who has been the go-between for heaven and men's minds, but who has employed 'the countenance and grace of Heaven' in rebellion against 'Heaven's substitute', the King. In reply, Scroop points out that the King's original rejection of the claim for redress of grievances had given birth to the armed rising. The Prince then suggests that the grievances shall be promptly redressed, and suggests that both armies be immediately discharged. Peace thus having been agreed to, Hastings goes off to discharge the rebel forces, while Westmoreland is sent, ostensibly, on the same mission to the royal troops.

Shouts of joy are heard without from the armies receiving the news, and the two groups of leaders drink together in happy celebration. But the rebel army is disbanded, while that of the Prince awaits orders, and the blow falls: the Archbishop, Mowbray and Hastings are seized and arrested as traitors. Mowbray questions the justice and honour of such an action, and the Archbishop demands, 'Will you thus break your faith?', to which Prince John, in reply, reminds the leaders that although he promised redress he did not promise to spare traitors, and gives orders for their immediate execution.

Scene three. During the ensuing skirmishes between Prince John's soldiers and parties of the rebels in flight, Falstaff arrives to join the royal forces and encounters *Sir John Coleville*, one of the rebel leaders. As they make ready to fight, Coleville recognizes his stout adversary by his huge stomach, and kneeling before Falstaff, surrenders without a fight.

While Falstaff is commenting on his own obesity, which, he tells his prisoner, impedes his agility, Prince John appears on the scene, accompanied by Westmoreland and Blunt. The Prince's anger at Falstaff's late arrival is somewhat blunted by the sight of the prisoner, whom Falstaff declares to be 'a most furious knight and valorous enemy', to which the Prince grudgingly replies, 'It was more of his courtesy than your deserving.' Falstaff adopts this version of the incident, comparing himself to Julius Caesar who came, saw, and conquered, and requests that the Prince include an account of how Coleville was captured in his report on the defeat of the rebels. The Prince promises to speak of Falstaff better than he deserves, gives him permission to return to London via Gloucestershire, gives Westmoreland instructions to send Coleville to York for immediate execution, and then makes his departure.

Left alone, Falstaff dilates on the virtues of sack: Prince John, he muses, has no sense of humour because he drinks no wine. Sherry, particularly, he declares, makes one forget troubles, warms the blood, and gives one courage. Thus, Falstaff concludes, if he had any sons of his own the first thing he would teach them would be 'to addict themselves to sack'.

Bardolph arrives with the news that the royal army is discharged, and Falstaff informs him of his resolve to revisit Shallow in Gloucestershire.

Scene four. In the Jerusalem Chamber of the Palace at Westminster the King, seated in his chair of state, and attended by his two younger sons, *Prince Thomas of Clarence* and *Prince Humphrey of Gloucester*, and the Earls of Warwick and Kent, declares that once the rebellions have been successfully crushed and he has regained his personal strength, he will head an expedition to the Holy Land, there to expiate the guilt of his usurpation.

The King then converses with his two sons Humphrey and Thomas concerning their brother Henry: Hal, he declares, is gracious, generous and sympathetic; yet he also has numerous faults, being quick-tempered, frivolous and moody. The King thus instructs Thomas (whom Henry loves more than any of his other brothers) to cherish Hal's affections and quietly to correct his faults. After he had died, concludes the King, Thomas must see that all his brothers act together and mould a strong monarchy under Hal. On hearing from Thomas that Prince Henry is dining in London with Poins and his other usual companions, the King is tortured with the spectre of Hal, when he is 'sleeping with (his) ancestors', ruling over England in a rash, headstrong, unguided manner. The Earl of Warwick, however, defends Prince Henry, who, he declares, merely frequents the haunts of London to learn from direct experience the manners and tastes of his people; in time, he will cast off his rough companions, yet be able to use his experiences in governing the country. To this the King replies that the Prince is as little likely to leave his evil companions as the bee the carrion where she has once lodged her comb.

This conversation is interrupted by the arrival of Westmoreland with the news that 'there is not now a rebel's sword unsheathed' in the north following on Prince John's great victory over Scroop, Hastings and Mowbray; he is soon followed by *Harcourt* with further good news – the Earl of Northumberland and Lord Bardolph have been completely routed by the Sheriff of Yorkshire.

But the King can only ask why such good news should make him sick, and confess 'now I am much ill'. He then swoons, falling on the floor. While Westmoreland and Warwick are reviving their monarch, the two princes discuss the omens which have recently manifested themselves, and which usually herald the death of kings. Henry then revives sufficiently to ask to carried gently to some other chamber. Warwick and Westmoreland carry him out, the Princes following.

Scene five. Some time later, in another chamber of the palace, the King falls asleep, having given Warwick previous instructions to place the crown on his pillow. Prince Hal enters the room, is somewhat taken aback to discover how ill his father has become, and remains in the chamber when Warwick and the Princes Thomas and Humphrey withdraw.

Prince Hal, sitting all alone at the bedside of his dying father, watching him as he sleeps, apostrophizes the crown, vowing that he will not be deprived of his birthright once his father is dead. As Hal draws nearer the bed, he believes his father to be dead, and the Prince is moved to place the crown on his own head. He kneels a moment in prayer, and then, stricken with grief, slowly carries the crown with him out of the chamber.

The King stirs, awakes, and, missing the crown, calls out for Warwick and his sons. While Warwick is sent to fetch Prince Hal, Henry is led bitterly to reflect on how sons can turn against their loving fathers in order to gain material advancement. Warwick returns with the news that he found the Prince in the next room sorrowfully washing his tear-stained cheeks. Hal himself then re-enters with the crown, cries out to his father, 'I never thought to hear you speak again', and then is left alone with the King as Warwick and the rest withdraw.

Henry, however, expresses grief as a father to think that his son was impatient for his decease, and bitterly reproaches Hal for his unfilial haste in removing the crown. He can see only misfortune for the state when the time comes for his son to put on the crown, and pictures his 'poor kingdom' administered by Hal's ruffian friends, who will 'commit the oldest sins' in 'the newest kind of ways'.

Declaring his complete innocence of any unworthy motives, Prince Hal again sets the crown on the pillow, and explains how, believing his father to be dead, he had removed the crown as a symbol of care; he protests his reluctance to succeed his father, and repeats to him the words he had spoken to the crown. After hearing this, the King forgives Hal, and a final reconciliation between them is effected.

The King proceeds to give to Hal his 'very latest counsel'. He briefly surveys the griefs and quarrels of his reign, and alludes to his successful liquidation of the men who helped him to power. He then confesses that the motive behind his frustrated plans to recover the Holy Sepulchre for Christendom was not wholly pious in its intention: he had intended to take his nobles to Jerusalem in order to prevent them from making trouble for him at home. The King confesses, too, that he has worn his crown with discomfort, yet he is certain that it can be worn with more assurance by his son, and that it will bring him greater happiness. Yet he feels that his heir is not yet firmly enough established, and he commends to Hal the expedience of establishing himself more firmly on the throne by exploiting the patriotism of his subjects in wars abroad.

The Prince echoes his father's hopes for the crown, and promises to maintain it "'Gainst all the world'. Prince John of Lancaster returns and greets his dying father. The King then summons Warwick and tells him of desire to be carried to the Jerusalem Chamber. He sees that the prophesy that he 'should not die but in Jerusalem' must be fulfilled less gloriously than he had hoped.

Act five

Scene one. Having meanwhile returned to Gloucestershire, Falstaff, accompanied by Bardolph and his page, is being made welcome by Justice Shallow in the hall of the latter's house. He presses Falstaff to stay over the night, and then, while Sir John sits and talks with Bardolph, calls for *Davy*, his servant, who comes from within.

Shallow gives Davy detailed instructions on how to prepare for their honoured guests, and whispers to him that he intends making use of Falstaff's friendship to gain personal advancement at court. Davy is thus instructed to treat Falstaff's men hospitably as well, and the servant finds great difficulty in securing Shallow's attention on matters of purely domestic routine.

Shallow and his servant then go to make preparation for their guests, while Bardolph and the page go out to attend to the horses. Falstaff, rising slowly, resolves, in soliloquy, to make laughter for Prince Hal 'out of Shallow'. whom he declares to be no better in spirit or character than the servants that he orders about. He muses that both Shallow and his servants have bad effects on one another.

Scene two. In a room in the Palace of Westminster, Warwick informs the Lord Chief Justice that King Henry IV is dead. The Judge is anxious for his own personal safety. The two are then joined by Prince Hal's three brothers and Westmoreland, all of whom frankly express gloomy anticipations about Prince Hal's policy once he has been crowned king. The Chief Justice is the most perturbed, for, having once been boxed on the ear by Prince Hal, he had sent him to prison for a short term. Nevertheless he will not ask for any pardon from the new king – he will allow events to take their course.

Prince Henry, accompanied by Blunt, then arrives on the scene with words of genial reassurance to his brothers: he assures them that he is not following the example of the Turkish sultan Amurath who strangled all possible claimants to the throne on his accession; the only need for sadness at the present time, continues Hal, is because of their joint grief over their dead father. Then, turning to the Lord Chief Justice, the young king momentarily drops his new demeanour to remind the judge of the 'great indignities' which he had laid upon 'the immediate heir of England'.

The Lord Chief Justice then points out that when he had imprisoned Hal, he had merely been doing his duty as administrator of the law; Prince Henry (as he then was) by striking him, the Chief Justice, had defied the authority of his father, Henry IV; and he asks Hal how he would feel if he had a son who showed no respect for the king's law. The Chief Justice, therefore, does not crave pardon for his action.

The Justice's noble vindication of his case leads to an equally noble reply from Hal: he honours the Chief Justice for his uprightness, graciously requests him to continue in his office, and asks him to employ his wisdom and experience in assisting the new regime, acting 'as a father to my youth'. Then, turning to his three brothers, Hal declares that his youthful wildness has now been buried and he intends governing the country with the assistance of the best administrators Parliament can offer. After his coronation he will summon his council and rule so effectively and wisely that none of his subjects will have cause to pray, 'God shorten Harry's happy life one day!'

Scene three. As yet, news of Henry IV's death has not reached Gloucestershire, where Falstaff, Bardolph and the page are being entertained by the justices Silence and Shallow in the latter's orchard, after having dined and wined. As Davy sets dishes of fruit and wine upon the table, Silence bursts into snatches of Bacchanalian ditties, and vows he has 'been merry twice and once ere now'. These songs draw ironical compliments from Falstaff, while the servant Davy, as he busies himself in serving the guests and plying them with wine, expresses a hope of seeing London once before he dies.

There is a sudden knocking from within; Davy goes to the door to return with Pistol, who has come from London with the news of the King's death. But he does not impart his news immediately: after fondly greeting Sir John, he is offended by Silence who compares Falstaff with 'goodman Puff of Barson'. Falstaff listens patiently to this fooling with Silence, but his obvious boredom immediately vanishes when Pistol at last declares that Henry IV is as dead 'as nail in door' and welcomes 'these pleasant days'.

Falstaff exclaims that he is 'fortune's steward' now that Prince Hal is king, and promises Pistol and Shallow that he will bestow them with high offices. Bardolph is sent to prepare their horses for an immediate return to London. Falstaff, Shallow and Pistol hurry inside, while Davy and other servants bring up the rear, carrying the drunken Silence up to bed.

Scene four. In a street in London two beadles are dragging Mistress Quickly and Doll Tearsheet to prison. One of the beadles explains to the hostess, who is struggling against this indignity, that Doll is the main culprit. Doll loudly reviles the beadles, who nevertheless carry her off to prison for a whipping as punishment for her part in a recent tavern brawl, where, in Falstaff's absence, she had been successful in provoking Pistol to bloodshed.

Scene five. In a public place near Westminster Abbey the new King and his coronation procession file past and enter the Abbey itself. A few moments later, Falstaff, Shallow, Pistol, Bardolph and the page, travel-stained and sweating after their swift night ride from Gloucestershire, take their places in the crowd. As they await the reappearance of the royal procession, Falstaff, who has borrowed a thousand pounds from Shallow, declares that he is now pleased he did not spend the money on fitting themselves out in new liveries, for he is convinced that their disorderly appearance will count to their advantage with the King as expressing the speed with which they have hastened to do honour to Hal, 'putting all affairs else in oblivion'. In melodramatic terms, Pistol relates the news of the arrests of Doll and Mistress Quickly, but Falstaff replies that he will have no difficulty about securing the release of the two women now that Hal is king.

There is a shout within the Abbey like the roaring of the sea, a clangour of trumpets, the doors open, and the coronation procession streams out. Crying out, 'God save thee, my sweet boy!', Falstaff thrusts past the King's guards, and confronts the new monarch. Hal sternly repudiates his past friendship, and declares, 'How ill white hairs become a fool and jester'; he calls upon Falstaff to leave his riotous habits and to carry himself gravely, as becomes his age. Yet he is prepared to grant Falstaff an allowance 'for the competence of life' so that he will not be forced into evil ways. But he gives him a solemn warning not to come within ten miles of the Palace, and commits him and his friends to the custody of the Chief Justice.

The royal procession then passes out of sight, but Falstaff and his friends remain. Sir John comforts himself with the thought that the King will send for him in private when night comes, and he will yet be able to make the fortunes of his friends. But Shallow, realizing that his chances of advancement have vanished, asks in vain for even five hundred of his thousand pounds.

Even as he speaks, the Chief Justice, accompanied by Prince John, returns, and gives the order to his officers that Falstaff and his friends are to be consigned to the fleet. Falstaff breaks out, 'My lord, my lord', but he is cut short and hurried away. Left alone with the Chief Justice, Prince John speaks with enthusiasm about the anticipated war with France.

Epilogue

A *Dancer* speaks the Epilogue, hinting at a continuation of the story, and making a definite promise that Falstaff will again figure prominently in the sequel. Using the language of a bankrupt debtor to his creditors who might send him to prison, the speaker asks pardon from the audience, and requests that they accept this indifferent play as part payment.

VII Shakespeare's dramatic style

Although *Henry IV, Part Two* resembles the other Chronicle Plays in a certain regality of tone which is seldom encountered elsewhere in Shakespeare, it contains special attributes of dramatic style which require individual discussion.

Lack of unity. There is an un-Shakespearian lack of unity in the plot structure of this part; we are presented with a series of events, very loosely strung together, with no mounting climax (unless the last interview between Hal and his father be regarded as such a climax), and with the events marching towards no determined end. Many of the scenes (such as Falstaff's 'recruiting campaign' and his capture of Coleville), while amusing in themselves, could be omitted without affecting the play as a whole.

Twin plots. Like many of Shakespeare's plays, *Henry IV, Part Two* contains more than one theme; there are two stories:

The serious story, which tells of the difficulties confronting Henry IV through the continuation of rebellion in England, his pricks of conscience at his own usurpation of the throne, and his anxiety for the reformation of Prince Hal.

The comic story, which is bound up with the activities of Falstaff and his associates at the Boar's Head Tavern and in Gloucestershire.

Prince Henry acts as a link between these twin plots, but, as his attitude changes after his father's death, so does the effectiveness of this function weaken, and the dramatist finds increasing difficulty in commingling the serious and comic elements.

The magnificent soliloquies. Much of the play's looseness of construction and many of its other defects in style are more than compensated by the dramatic richness and poetic feeling of the important soliloquies, of which the leading examples are:

By Falstaff when he sees to the bottom of Shallow (Act three, scene two) and when he dilates on the virtues of wine (Act Four, scene three).

By Prince Hal when he bitterly reflects on his past mode of life and present companions (Act two, scene two), and when he addresses the crown at his father's deathbed (Act four, scene five).

By King Henry IV when he is outworn with sleeplessness (Act three, scene one) and when he muses on the unfilial behaviour of sons (Act four, scene five).

These soliloquies, whether comic (as those of Falstaff) or highly tragic (as those of the King) are written in sonorous, simple diction, depicting the characters of their speakers with unfailing consistency.

A social document. Unlike many of Shakespeare's other 'histories', *Henry IV, Part Two* is not content with a dramatic account of life on one social plane: the picture given the audience of the period lies along several horizontal and vertical planes. We are taken behind the scenes at Court and move just as easily among the high-born rebels in their camp. Then we are transported to the seamier side of London life, and, with Falstaff, we hear 'the chimes at midnight' while the merriment continues at Mistress Quickly's tavern. At Master Shallow's in rural Gloucestershire we 'eat a last year's pippin of my own grafting, with a dish of caraways, and so forth', only to be whisked away to the battlefront or to witness a Coronation spectacle. And yet, although the dramatist's eyes seem to have roamed everywhere, these various scenes of English life at different levels are so skilfully arranged that they do not distract the audience's mind from the main thread of the historical drama.

Preference for Prince Hal. 'Show me your friends and I will tell you what sort of man you are', is as true of Shakespeare as of anybody else. Thus, although Shakespeare always stands aloof from his characters, there is one character in this drama that stands out, most patently, as being his favourite – the one whom he most admired and fashioned with a creator's understanding of his creature's weaknesses and strengths – namely, Prince Hal, later to become King Henry V.

Whether he plays the fool with Falstaff, is given over to fits of despondency and disillusionment, or excuses himself to his father, Shakespeare is with him all the time, watching him like a guardian angel, condoning his folly, exulting in his prowess. The young Prince is the only one who can successfully measure wits with Falstaff, and, whenever he appears, Shakespeare always gives him the best lines. There seems little doubt that Prince Hal was one of Shakespeare's boyhood heroes.

Shakespeare's interpretation of history. From the five acts which Shakespeare uses to portray the latter part of the reign of King Henry IV, practically everything of historical importance is excluded as irrelevant to the theme with which Shakespeare is dealing here. Futhermore, Shakespeare compresses the events of almost two decades into a short space of time, while three separate rebellions become two phases of a single rebellion against the King. (See the section of Characterization in these notes.) Two other significant changes have been made by Shakespeare: Henry's proposed visit to the Holy Land had, in actual fact, little real connection with the death of Richard II or with Henry's desire to make expiation, while the King's worry over Prince Hal is much exaggerated by Shakespeare, and the acceptance by the King of his son's misdeeds as divine retribution for his own sins is the dramatist's own interpretation. Yet all these changes by the dramatist to the historical chronicles have the effect of enhancing the movement, atmosphere and interest of the play.

Some other faults. It has already been mentioned that lack of effective unity is the drama's most obvious defect. There are other, though minor, blemishes. In no other Shakespearian play of the same length are there so many characters. This creates less confusion when the play is actually performed on the stage (except, perhaps, in the instance of the two Bardolphs) than when it is read for study. Another fault lies in the very minor roles played by the female characters; even the most important of the women – Mistress Quickly – is never allowed to dominate more than half a scene. Finally, most of the rebel leaders as well as the King's advisers (including the Lord Chief Justice and Warwick) deliver themselves too often in the style of set speeches rather than as flesh-and-blood creations stirred by real emotions.

VIII Characterization

As far as character development is concerned, *Henry IV, Part Two* is chiefly bound up, on the one hand, with the leading of Prince Henry back from the path of error, and, on the other hand, with the ruin of Falstaff. Thus, despite the title of the drama, the young Prince and Falstaff emerge as the two major characters, while King Henry IV plays a relatively minor part.

The major features of Prince Henry's character
Prince Henry was evidently a great favourite with Shakespeare, who builds him up as a popular figure of a young scapegrace who suddenly betters expectation and surprises the world with his wisdom, magnanimity and success.

Zest for life. Henry undoubtedly enjoys the low life of Eastcheap. His plea that he consorts with low companions merely in order that he may surprise the world later on with a timely reformation is a rationalization of his conduct and an easy way of finding a good and sufficient reason for doing what he wants to do. Prince Hal, when he finds a good excuse to think well of himself, does not easily let it go. Thus he holds fast to the pious assumption that, in amusing himself with Falstaff, he is preparing to stagger society with a well-timed reformation and that he is in the meantime collecting useful information and experience. Shakespeare leaves us to decide for ourselves how far Henry really conducts himself according to plan, or how far he is merely creating an alibi for his misdemeanours.

Filial piety. In the first scene in which Henry appears in the Second Part of *King Henry IV*, direct reference is made to another leading motive of the play. The King is sick and the Prince is believed by many to be waiting for his father's crown. Rather than rest under such an imputation, Hal unbosoms himself to a companion (Poins) whom he despises and cannot refrain from insulting. But his tenderness of filial piety appears fully in his genuine grief at his father's last sickness; and his virtuous prudence no less appears in his avoiding all show of grief, as he knows that this, taken together with his past levity, will be sure to draw on him the imputation of hypocrisy.

Making use of others for his own ends. But if we follow Shakespeare and look a bit more closely at the Prince, we discover with the many fine traits a few less pleasing. King Henry IV describes him as the noble image of his own youth; and, for all his superiority over his father, he is still his father's son, and is equally willing to use other people as a means to his own ends which is a conspicuous feature in his father. Thus he never speaks of Falstaff to Poins with any real affection. The truth is that the members of the family of Henry IV have love for one another, but they cannot spare love for anyone outside their family, which stands firmly united, defending its royal position against attack and instinctively isolating itself from outside influence.

Moral upliftment. But the drama remains basically an historical play, in the course of which the Prince's finer qualities were to be gradually revealed. Thus Shakespeare separates the Prince from Falstaff as much as he can, withdrawing him from Falstaff's influence, and weakening in the audience's mind the connection between the two. In the first part of the play they are constantly together; in the second, they are together only once before the rejection. Further, in the scenes where Hal appears apart from Falstaff, we watch him growing more and more grave, and awakening more and more poetic interest; while Falstaff, though his humour remains unflaggingly zestful, becomes increasingly coarse.

Respect for law and authority. As the higher elements of the Prince's nature are called forth and there is a gradual sundering of the ties that bind him to Falstaff, so he clearly indicates that, even in his wildest excesses, he has drunk deeply of the fountain of truth and wisdom. This is nowhere more clearly displayed than when, immediately after his father's death, he encounters the Chief Justice, who has strong reasons to fear the worst on Hal's accession. Instead, the new king honours the Chief Justice for his uprightness, and displays a keen awareness and respect for the authority of the law.

Few characters in Shakespeare have met with more divergent

criticism than Prince Henry: it is, however, difficult in many cases to gather whether it is the man, as depicted, who is censured, or Shakespeare for so depicting him.

The development of Prince Henry's character

The Prince first appears on his return from Wales in company with Poins. His general attitude appears to have changed very little: he is familiar as before with his dissolute companions, and interchanges with them his coarse and indelicate witticisms. But here, for the first time, he is ashamed of this low taste, and reproaches himself for associating with Poins and his friends. At the same time, the thought of his father's sickness and possible death has softened him, and his heart bleeds inwardly; yet intercourse with his frivolous companions has made him unaccustomed to sorrow and sadness. Poins believes this to be hypocrisy, and looks upon his former hilarity at the prospect of the crown as his true attitude. This arouses the princely blood in Henry: 'Thou think'st me', he says to Poins, 'as far in the devil's book as thou and Falstaff for obduracy and persistency; let the end try the man.'

In the same scene he receives letters from Falstaff in the old familiar tone, but in the manner in which he receives them, and in the manner in which he converses with Poins, a separation of feeling is perceptible. The seriousness of the northern rebellion, the illness of his father, the approach of his accession all serve to ripen into action the resolutions of his opening soliloquy. He can no longer, with his irresistible humour, resign himself as before to the frivolities of his old friends. 'We play the fool with the time', he says, 'and the spirits of the wise sit in the clouds and mock us.' He enquires after Falstaff, he wishes to go in disguise to spy on him, but he is not going mainly to seek diverting pleasure; there is an object in his errand – he wants to see Falstaff in his true colours.

Prince Henry finds Falstaff heartlessly mocking him in the hearing of the reprobate Doll Tearsheet. This backbiting appears to the Prince to go beyond jest, and an inner estrangement between the two is felt throughout the scene. There is very little comedy in the exchanges between the two major characters, and when the tidings come from Court, the freely indulged mirth of former times does not reappear.

The Prince comes to court at his father's end. The King's apparent death cuts him to the heart, and Warwick finds him sitting over the crown like a picture of 'mourning sorrow'. After the King's death, the hearts even of the most unconcerned tremble with doubt as to what the kingdom may expect from him. But his brothers see with astonishment Henry's deep emotion when he appears as King; the Lord Chief Justice is kept in suspense until at the very last Henry calmly sets all at rest by promising that the very man who had him imprisoned shall be a father to him, and that he will follow his wise directions, since wildness and passion have died and been buried with his father.

The final rejection of Falstaff (see below) rounds off the complete change in the Prince's character, and prepares the audience for his great military exploits in the ensuing play.

Falstaff – 'A marvellous congregation of charms and vices'

Falstaff's distinction lies in the abundance of his ludicrous traits. Shakespeare skilfully makes his audience laugh at a man with a huge belly and corresponding appetites: at the incongruity of his unwieldy bulk and the nimbleness of his spirit; at the large-scale lies he tells and the suddenness of their exposure and frustration. But while these incongruities are quite essential to Falstaff's character, there is much more to him than that.

His happy spirit. The main reason why Falstaff makes his audiences so happy is that he puts them entirely at their ease since he himself is always entirely at ease. Enjoyment is the keynote of all his actions: and this enjoyment lies chiefly in eating and drinking, taking his ease at the inn, and in merry companionship. There is little doubt, also that Falstaff makes himself out to be more ludicrous than he is, in order that he and others may laugh. It is he who says that he walks before his page 'like a sow that hath o'erwhelmed all her litter but one'. And he jests at himself when he is alone just as much as when others are present.

His contagious enjoyment. For all his addiction to wine, Falstaff's brain seems never dulled by it, nor does he become solemn, silly, pious or quarrelsome. The 'virtue' it instils into him, of filling his brain with nimble, fiery and delectable shapes, and his humorous attitude, free him from slavery to it. And it is this freedom, and no secret longing for better things, that makes his enjoyment of life so contagious.

Enemy of all things serious. But Falstaff's happy spirit is not only directed against obvious absurdities – he is also the enemy of everything that would interfere with his ease, and therefore anything serious, and especially of everything respectable and moral. Thus he makes *truth* appear absurd by solemn statements which he utters with perfect gravity and which he expects nobody to believe. At the same time, *law* is reduced by him to absurdity through evading all the attacks of its highest representative and almost forcing the latter to laugh at his own defeat. *Patriotism* is made ridiculous when he fills his pockets with the bribes offered by competent soldiers who want to escape service, while he takes instead the maimed and the useless. And *courage* he makes absurd by mocking at his own capture of Coleville. He performs these achievements, not with the sourness of a cynic, but with the frivolity of a youth.

Effect on companions. No other character in the drama seems fully to understand Falstaff. Mrs Quickly and Bardolph are both enslaved by his personality, but neither knows why. 'Well, fare thee well', says the hostess whom he has pillaged and forgiven. 'I have known thee these twenty-nine years, come peas-cod time, but an honester and true-hearted man – well, fare thee well.'

Contempt for public opinion. Both Poins and the Prince get Falstaff into corners for the pleasure of seeing him escape in ways they cannot imagine. But they both often take him much too seriously. Poins, for instance, rarely sees, and the Prince does not always see, that when Falstaff speaks ill of a companion behind his back, or writes to the Prince that Poins spreads it abroad that the Prince is to marry his sister, he knows quite well that what he says will be repeated, and is absolutely indifferent whether it is repeated or not, so long as it gives him further opportunities for enjoyment.

The purpose of his lies. It is the same with his lying. He tells lies either for their own humour, or with the specific intention of getting himself into difficulties. He rarely expects to be believed, and abandons statements or contradicts them the moment they are uttered. Thus there is not more intent in his lying than there is in the humorous exaggerations which he pours out in soliloquy when he is alone. This attitude is partly understood by Poins and the Prince: they wait eagerly – disguised as drawers – to convict him; not to put him to shame, but in order to enjoy the greater lie that will swallow up the lesser! Thus Falstaff was hardly in earnest when, wanting to get twenty-two yards of satin on trust from Master Dombledon the silk-mercer, he offered Bardolph as security; or when he said to the Chief Justice about Mistress Quickly, who accused him of breaking his promise to marry her, 'My Lord, this is a poor mad soul, and she says up and down the town that her eldest son is like you.' There is nothing serious in any of these statements except Falstaff's refusal to take anything seriously.

His alleged cowardice. There is no denying the fact that Falstaff sometimes behaves in a cowardly manner, but that does not necessarily mean that he is a cowardly spirit. On the contrary, this disproved by the opinions of some of the other characters and by the actions of Falstaff himself.

Shallow, for instance, remembers him fifty-five years ago breaking Scogan's head at the court-gate 'when he was a crack not thus high', and he remembers him later as a good backsword man.

But even during the action of the play itself Falstaff remains a person of importance to the army, and Peto relates how twelve captains are hurrying about London searching for him.

The messenger who brings the false report of the battle to Northumberland, when the drama opens, mentions, as one of the important incidents, the death of Sir John Falstaff.

Coleville, expressly described as a famous rebel, surrenders to him as soon as he hears his name, although he had boldly confronted Coleville and was quite ready to fight with him.

To draw upon Pistol and force him downstairs in the Tavern and wound him in the shoulder was no great feat, but an abject coward would have shrunken from it.

Personal pride. Nevertheless, Falstaff does not entirely discard everything he professes to ridicule. He shows a certain pride in his rank, and is by no means indifferent to reputation: when the Chief Justice asks him to pay his debt to the Hostess for his reputation's sake, he certainly feels a twinge of conscience. It is also very significant that, for all his dissolute talk, he never allows the Prince or others of his respected friends to see him behaving in an immoral manner.

Affection for the Prince. Another aspect of his personality which he cannot disguise under his humour is his genuine affection for his friends – especially for Bardolph – and his overwhelming love for the young Prince. However hard he tries, he cannot jest this love out of existence, and when he greets Hal after the coronation there is a genuine warmth and pleasure in the greeting; so, too, is this affection apparent from his remarks on discovering the Prince's identity at the tavern.

His perennial poverty. A consequence of Falstaff's love for constant entertainment and good living is that he cannot eat and drink for ever without money; his purse consequently suffers from consumption, and when the Chief Justice tells him that his means are very slender and his waste great, he puns the answer, 'I would it were otherwise; I would my means were greater and my waist slenderer.'

The seamy side. His lack of money motivates Falstaff's evil actions which are perfectly consistent with the other side of his character. He cheats his tailor, he fleeces Justice Shallow, he defies the Chief Justice because his position as an officer in service gives him power to do wrong; finally, the dangerous, wholly irresponsible side of his personality is strongly emphasized in his last words as he hurries from Shallow's house to London: 'Let us take any man's horses; the laws of England are at my commandment; happy are they that have been my friends, and woe unto my lord Chief Justice.'

Yet, despite the obnoxious side to Falstaff's character, he is perhaps 'the greatest triumph of the comic Muse that the world has to show' (Hudson).

The final rejection of Falstaff by King Henry V

After considering the characters of King Henry V (Prince Hal) and Falstaff, one is left with an important dilemma: if the Falstaff scenes have been enjoyed as keenly as Shakespeare obviously meant them to be enjoyed, and Falstaff is regarded as a supreme comic rather than a ruffian, then a certain amount of astonishment is bound to be felt at Prince Hal's (not King Henry V's) curt rejection of his old companion, while there is certain to be resentment at the subsequent return of the Chief Justice, who sends Falstaff to prison. Now why did Shakespeare end his drama with a scene which leaves an impression so unpleasant?

Of course it can be argued that Shakespeare intended his audiences to regard Falstaff with indignation and disgust, that they would naturally feel nothing but pleasure at his downfall. Such an argument completely disregards the inner qualities of the dramatist's characterization, and deserves no further comment.

A more ingenious suggestion is that Falstaff, having listened to the King's speech, did not seriously hope to be sent for by him in private; thus, by turning to Shallow after the King's departure and declaring, 'I owe you a thousand pounds', Sir John is able to display his humorous superiority to the rebuff, and so prove himself inwardly undefeated. But this argument wholly ignores Falstaff's subsequent dismissal to the fleet, while the circumstances of his death in *King Henry V* (since, in the words of Hostess Quickly, 'The King has killed his heart') clearly indicate that Shakespeare intended Falstaff's rejection to be regarded in its true light as a catastrophe.

Now the development of Prince Hal's character throughout *King Henry IV, Part II* indicates that it was inevitable that, on his accession, the new King would completely cut himself off from Falstaff's influence. It is not surprising, then, that Harry permanently banishes Falstaff ten miles beyond his own royal presence. But such arrangements could have been carried out with great humour and need not have prevented a satisfactory ending to the play. Yet if the character of Prince Henry is correctly interpreted, this display of hardness by the new monarch should come as no surprise. If the more unpleasant side of Henry's character is kept in mind, the incident of Falstaff's banishment becomes clearer: after he had left Falstaff in the final scene, it is highly conceivable that Henry was meant to give way to anger at the familiarity with which Falstaff had addressed him during the Coronation procession, in the presence of the Court and the London onlookers; he thus sent the Chief Justice back to take vengeance.

But this explanation does not really solve the problem, for there is still a feeling of resentment against Henry. It would therefore seem that Shakespeare must have intended that the audience's sympathies with Falstaff would have been so far weakened by this stage to make Falstaff's discomfiture satisfactory, and that the audience should approve the moral judgement that falls on him. Consequently, in creating the character of Falstaff, the dramatist apparently overshot the mark: he created such an extraordinary personality and fixed him so firmly in the audience's affections, that when he sought to dethrone him, his efforts failed. Thus, although the audience wishes

Henry a successful reign, its sympathies go with Falstaff to the fleet.

The character of King Henry IV

The character of King Henry IV is worked out by Shakespeare with shrewd penetration, although, as already mentioned, despite the drama's title the King can only be regarded as the third major character.

Crafty politician. Shakespeare represents King Henry IV as an unscrupulous politician, skilful alike at penetrating others' designs and at concealing his own. For one of the King's main peculiarities is that he looks solely to results; and, the better to secure these, he keeps his designs and processes in the dark. He would gladly divert all political opposition by leading an expedition to the Holy Land. In dying, he bequeathes to his son the lesson of his domestic policy: that he should 'busy giddy minds with foreign quarrels; that action, hence borne out, may waste the memory of the former days' (i.e. the memory of how he had acquired the throne). Thus, political craftiness is the leading trait of King Henry IV.

Wise statesmanship. Political cunning is nevertheless not so prominent but that other and better traits are strongly visible. And even in his political policy there is much of breadth and largeness which distinguishes the statesman from the politician. In many of his utterances it becomes clear that he has a real eye to the interests of his country (although the interest of his family are always placed first). Even in his last talk to Prince Hal a kernel of moral sense is revealed beneath his close-knit prudence.

Shrewd penetration. Henry's perfect self-command over his emotions, which have no impulsive gushes or starts, is in great part the secret of his strange power over others. He has the same sharp insight of men as of means: even when outworn with sleeplessness, he is able to penetrate the schemes of the Northumberland rebels and give instructions accordingly.

His guilty conscience. But the King's last actions and speeches are strongly influenced by prophecy, superstition, and conscience – which are in strong contrast to his readiness, consistency and firmness in dealing with the rebels. Thus when his last adversaries are crushed, and his good fortune might have reached its prime, he is broken down by affliction, pain and inward distress. He sees in all this the punishment of God. His afflicted mind is most afflicted when, at the height of his good fortune, he can find neither peace nor rest. From the depths of his soul the lament arises (act three, scene one) that 'with all appliances and means to boot' he finds not that sleep which 'upon the high and giddy mast seals up the shipboy's eyes'. The presentiment overtakes him that generation after generation shall rise and continue the internal strife and war.

Attitude towards Prince Hal. Agitated as he is by scruples of conscience, King Henry is tormented further when he imagines that Prince Hal is lost in youthful dissolution and is unworthy of the throne. At the same time, on his deathbed, he believes that he has proof of the Prince's heartlessness and scheming. When Hal's explanation quiets and convinces him, and lightens his dying hour, he at length unveils his true character, acknowledging the by-paths and crooked ways he has trodden to attain the crown, and he sees his dignity and right to the throne resting alone in a proper care of the state, and not in hereditary possessions.

(Note: According to the chronicler Holinshed, Prince Hal had good reason for believing his father to be dead, for the attendants had 'covered his face with a linen cloth'.)

Shallow and Silence
The two country Justices, Shallow and Silence, are admirably fitted to each other: Shallow highly appreciates his kinsman, who in turn looks up to him as a kind of superior being. We are introduced to them in their piece of dialogue about 'old Double', as if Shakespeare wanted his audience not to display too much contempt towards these two highly interesting characters.

The character of Shallow. Justice Shallow is vastly proud of his acquaintance with Sir John, while Falstaff is drawn to him quite as much for the pleasure of making fun of him as in the hope of emptying his purse.

One of Shallow's most serious blemishes is the exultant self-complacency with which he remembers his youthful escapades, although, in actual fact, and without his suspecting it, he had been the sport and butt of his companions. His reminiscences are therefore all the more diverting.

Another choice feature of Shallow is his habit of talking when he really has nothing to say. Thus when Falstaff asks to be excused from staying with him overnight, he replies: 'I will not excuse you; you shall not be excused; excuses shall not be admitted: there is no excuse shall serve; you shall not be excused.' And he lingers upon his words and keeps rolling them over in his mouth with a still keener relish in the orchard after supper. This fondness for meaningless repetition springs not merely from a shallow brain, but partly also from that vivid self-appreciation which causes him to dwell with such rapture on the 'spirited escapades' of his youth.

Another point in Shallow's make-up is his loquacious thinness, as is well instanced in his appreciation of Sir John's remark about Mouldy, one of the potential recruits (act three, scene two, lines 107–110). Of course, Shallow is more pleased with his own appreciation of the joke than with the joke itself.

Thus Shallow is a braggart, a liar, and a rogue, who betrays his poverty of thought in the chattering repetition of indifferent words. Having intended to use Falstaff at Court for his own advantage, the loquacious, brain blockhead falls an easy victim to the quick-witted, ironical Sir John.

But in this rural society, Shallow is not the lowest on the scale; he even possesses an admirer in his cousin Silence.

The character of Silence. Shallow's habit of bubbling meaningless phrases has almost certainly grown as a result of talking to his taciturn cousin and getting no replies!

For Silence is a person of asinine dullness, 'a stupendous platitude of a man', who has scarce life enough to carry on a conversation, unless it be to echo a question.

Yet there is a tremendous contrast between Silence dry and Silence drunk. Only excess of wine can stir his emotions, when his natural sterility of brain is overcome by the influence of sack on his memory, and he keeps pouring forth snatches from old ballads, to be finally carried off to bed.

(It is believed that the original of Justice Shallow was Sir Thomas Lucy (1532–1600), a Warwickshire squire, who is traditionally thought to have prosecuted Shakespeare for poaching; but no counterpart of Silence is known to have existed in real life.)

Falstaff's other associates

Bardolph Regarded by the Hostess as an 'arrant malmsey-nose' rogue, Bardolph is more Falstaff's servant than his associate, and is consequently very much of a passive character in this play. He comes off the worst in his exchange of banter with the page (act two, scene two), and is quite clearly aping his master when, on hearing of the King's death, he declares that he 'would not take a knighthood for his fortune'. However, there is no denying Bardolph's constant devotion and loyalty to Falstaff.

Pistol A bully and swaggerer by profession, Pistol is regarded as too shabby and disreputable even by the lowly, vice-ridden Doll Tearsheet. Unlike Falstaff, who is a mine of genuine wit, Pistol speaks with bombast and affectation in pompous phrases gathered from miserable tragedies. His is an over-fantastic character, or rather a distorted caricature from another world.

Poins Like Bardolph, Poins plays a passive role, although his short appearances reveal a man of somewhat superior intelligence compared to Falstaff's other associates; in this play, however, Poins is more a companion to the Prince than to Falstaff. He converses intimately with Hal (act three, scene two), who treats him familiarly, but with some contempt, while he is subsequently mentioned (act four, scene four) to the King as one of the Prince's 'continual followers'.

Mistress Quickly The play offers several glimpses of Mistress Quickly the hostess of Eastcheap, who can think of things only in the precise order of their occurrence, and who has no power to select fact to suit her purpose. Despite her mental passiveness and her numerous vices and vulgarities, her character is not unrelieved by traits of generosity and kindness, as is well shown in her treatment of Falstaff. Certainly, she gets wrought up to a pretty high pitch of temper, but she cannot hold herself there. Yet, despite the simplicity of her character, she displays considerable knowledge of the world, and is not without shrewdness: thus, when the beadles interfere after a murder has been committed in her tavern, she quickly raises a lamentation that 'right should thus overcome might', and wishes Falstaff back to help her.

Doll Tearsheet Described by Falstaff's page as 'a proper gentle woman ... and a kinswoman of my master's', Doll really represents one of the coarser sides of London social life. She is a prostitute with a sharp tongue and a strong taste for liquor, who, for being involved in a tavern brawl, is finally hauled to prison, loudly reviling the beadles. Yet even Doll is not without a softer side to her character. For instance, she has genuine affection for Falstaff, and bids him a tearful farewell when he leaves for the north.

The Page Falstaff's diminutive page, who has been placed in Sir John's service by Prince Hal to exert a good influence, instead of being able to improve his master, is soon so far influenced himself that although 'there is a good angel about him the devil outbids him too'. He cannot forbear a jest at Bardolph's expense, and is rewarded by the Prince for his gibes at Bardolph. The little page is undoubtedly intelligent, but extremely precocious.

Members of the rebel camp
As pointed out in the section of these notes on 'Shakespeare's interpretation of history' there are marked differences between Shakespeare's account of the rebellions during the reign of King Henry IV and the description given by the chronicler Holinshed. Holinshed recalls that after the battle of Shrewsbury in 1404, the Earl of Northumberland made a convenient peace with King Henry; that a second rebellion was initiated by Northumberland, Archbishop Scroop, and Mowbray, and was undertaken the next year, the Archbishop and the Earl Marshal being tricked into submission, while Northumberland escaped to Scotland and afterwards to Glendower in Wales; and that a third rebellion was led by Northumberland from Scotland, where he had returned after having gone to Flanders and France to seek aid. Northumberland was slain in battle with the Sheriff of Yorkshire before the King's forces had time to arrive to put down this third rebellion. Shakespeare has therefore combined these three rebellions into one, making it the major concern of the latter years of King Henry IV's reign.

Northumberland The Earl of Northumberland emerges as a man of resolute decisions which are never backed by action. On hearing of his son's death he feels a paroxysm of courage at the moment of rage and sorrow, but soon returns to his normal inactivity by a woman's arguments; instead of marching his troops he sends a letter to the Archbishop of York, as he had before done to Hotspur; and as he had left the one, so he now leaves the other to destruction and flees to Scotland.

Lady Percy Hotspur's widow and Northumberland's daughter-in-law, while devoted to the memory of her slain husband, is nevertheless not estranged from the earl; she displays strong powers of persuasion, using both emotional and objective arguments to induce him to seek safety in Scotland and desert the rebel cause.

Scroop, Archbishop of York Among the minor historical characters in the drama, that of the Archbishop is a noble portrait. He is forthright in speech, enterprising in purpose, and resolute in action. His main failing, which flows directly from his nobility of character, is that he places too much faith in his fellow beings. Having trusted Northumberland to bring reserves for the rebel army, his trust is shattered. Thereafter, he somewhat naïvely falls into Prince John's cunning trap. Yet throughout the disaster in Gaultree Forest, he remains grave, calm and dignified.

Lord Bardolph Like Scroop, Bardolph is shrewd, sensible and of a firm practical understanding; his cool judgement induces him to look carefully before he leaps, but, as events turn out, he was not careful enough! He is one of the strongest supporters of the rebel movement, and, on learning the truth about the disaster at Shrewsbury, he urges renewed efforts, first from Northumberland and then from the Archbishop. Yet he refuses to encounter the King's forces unprepared, and at the council of war advocates the postponement of operations until Northumberland's help is available.

Mowbray Perhaps the staunchest of the rebel group is Lord Mowbray. At the council of war in the Archbishop's palace (act one, scene three he has little information to offer, but he constantly urges immediate action against the royal forces. Later, at Gaultree, he recites his grievances of Henry to Westmoreland, and openly declares his distrust of Prince John's offer to hold a round-table discussion. Thus the somewhat impulsive Mowbray emerges as a shrewd judge of character, only to be treacherously seized while parleying with Prince John and sent with the other rebels 'to the block of death'.

The King's party
Of the King's supporters and followers, only three characters are worth special mention.

Prince John of Lancaster According to Falstaff, Prince Hal's younger brother has little sense of humour because he drinks no wine and eats only fish. In fact, Sir John fails in his efforts to move the Prince to laughter. To this gravity must be added strong attachment to his father's cause, a love of battle for its own sake, an ability to inspire confidence (even among his enemies), and, as a result thereof, an ability to use cunning and treachery to gain his objectives. There is much of his father's personality, therefore in the character of Prince John.

The Lord Chief Justice Besides the noble figure he makes at the close of the drama when he resolves that he will not crave pardon from Henry V for an action he rightfully committed, the Chief Justice is introduced on several occasions in verbal duels with Falstaff; in these his good-natured wisdom is clearly shown, while his suppressed enjoyment of the fat old sinner's wit serves to relieve, without modifying, the reverence due to his high office.

Earl of Warwick The Earl of Warwick is King Henry IV's constant adviser and attendant. He eases the King's fears about the recurrence of rebellion and subsequently palliates the light conduct of Prince Henry. Yet he completely misinterprets Hal's intentions, for he warns the Chief Justice that the new King loves him not. There is little doubt, however, about his genuine attachment and loyalty to King Henry IV, or about the sincerity of his anxiety for the King's health and personal welfare.

IX Revision exercises

The revision exercises which follow are not to be regarded as likely 'spot' questions.

1 Choose *eight* of the following extracts and for each extract state (a) by whom, to whom, and under what circumstances each was spoken, and (b) explain the general meaning of the extract and its special significance to the plot:

   (i) If I had a thousand sons, the first human principle I would teach them should be, to foreswear thin potations and to addict themselves to sack.
   (ii) Death, as the Psalmist saith, is certain to all; all shall die. How a good yoke of bullocks at Stamford fair?
   (iii) ... Commit
   The oldest sins the newest kind of ways.
   (iv) Yet the first bringer of unwelcome news
   Hath but a losing office, and his tongue
   Sounds ever after as a sullen bell,
   Remember'd knelling a departing friend.
   (v) Pray ... that our armies join not in a hot day; for, by the Lord, I take but two shirts out with me, and I mean not to sweat extraordinarily.
   (vi) How ill white hairs become a fool and jester.
   (vii) Thou didst swear to me upon a parcel-gilt goblet, sitting in my Dolphin-chamber, at the round table, by a sea-coal fire, upon Wednesday in Wheesonweek.
   (viii) Thus we play the fools with the time, and the spirits of the wise sit in the clouds and mock us.
   (ix) Uneasy lies the head that wears a crown.
   (x) Thy wish was father, Harry, to that thought.
   (xi) I may justly say, with the hook-nosed fellow of Rome, 'I came, saw, and overcame'.

(xii) ... When we mean to build,
We first survey the plot, then draw the model;
And when we see the figure of the house,
Then we must rate the cost of the erection.
(xiii) You lie in your throat if you say I am any other than an honest man.
(xiv) I were better to be eaten to death with a rust than to be scoured to nothing with perpetual motion.
(xv) ... O sleep, O gentle sleep,
Nature's soft nurse, how have I frighted thee,
That thou no more wilt weigh my eyelids down
And steep my senses in forgetfulness?

2 'Nothing that Prince Henry does makes an impression on Falstaff's insensible nature; all that the Prince contrives for him dissatisfies him; we see him fighting and quarrelling in the streets with a low woman whom he means to cheat and to dupe; we hear him with secret backbiting slandering his Lord, while in secret he swears destruction to the Chief Justice. Thus, instead of restoring his honour, he damages it further.'

Discuss the validity of the above comment on Falstaff's character.

3 Compare and contrast the characters of Prince Henry and Prince John, and show clearly how each reacts to the witty sallies of Falstaff.

4 Discuss *three* of the following (about 15 lines on each):

(i) The use of poetry and prose in *King Henry IV, Part II*;
(ii) Northumberland's character;
(iii) Shakespeare's perversion of history;
(iv) Falstaff's 'capture' of Coleville;
(v) The discussion by Bardolph and Shallow on the term 'accommodated' (act three, scene two).

5 Discuss *two* of the following (about 20-25 lines on each):

(i) The parts played by Warwick and Westmoreland in the play;
(ii) The contrast between Shallow and Silence;
(iii) Falstaff's 'recruits'.

6 Write an accurate account of Falstaff's first encounter with the

Lord Chief Justice in a London street, stressing particularly how Sir John's wit manages to turn the table on the grave official. What are the fundamental differences between this scene and Falstaff's final encounter with the Chief Justice?

7 'The drama contains several symptoms of a new energy preparing itself in the character of Prince Henry.'

Give an account of the development of Prince Henry's personality, showing clearly his motives for the final rejection of Falstaff.

8 (a) Describe the parts played by Archbishop Scroop, Lady Percy, and Mistress Quickly in the drama.
(b) Write a critical character analysis of King Henry IV.

9 If you were invited to take part in a stage presentation of *King Henry IV, Part II*, what character would you choose? Give reasons for your choice.

10 Discuss the character of Prince Henry from the following aspects:
   (i) his association with Falstaff;
   (ii) his relationship with his father;
   (iii) his attitude on ascending the throne.

11 *Henry IV, Part II* is a play in which there is a serious side and a humorous side. Give a clear summary of the humorous aspect of the drama, showing briefly how it is related to the serious aspect.

12 *Either* (a) give an account of the death-bed scene between Prince Henry and King Henry IV, *or* (b) describe fully the scene at the Boar's Head Tavern at Eastcheap.

Key to question one
The first lines in each of the fifteen quotations in question one are derived from the following acts and scenes:

(i) IV iii 119; (ii) III ii 35; (iii) IV v 126; (iv) I i 100; (v) I ii 204; (vi) V iv 48; (vii) II i 85; (viii) II ii 139; (ix) III i 31; (x) IV v 93; (xi) IV iii 39; (xii) I iii 41; (xiii) I ii 79; (xiv) I ii 212; (xv) III i 5

X Bibliographical note

Popular texts
King Henry IV, Part II has been published in a number of annotated editions. Detailed notes and commentaries will be found in the *Arden Shakespeare* (edited by Winstanley) and in the *Tutorial Shakespeare* series (edited by Collins).

Biographies of Shakespeare
The two standard works on the life of Shakespeare are those of Sir Sidney Lee (Macmillan, 1925), and Joseph Quincey Adams (Houghton Mifflin, 1923). An interesting study of Shakespeare's surroundings and a scrutiny of fact and tradition about him will be found in J. S. Smart's *Shakespeare: Truth and Tradition* (Longmans, 1928). Sir Walter Raleigh's *Shakespeare* in the 'Pocket Library' (Macmillan, 1907) is still a scholarly but essentially readable biography.

Books on the Elizabethan age
The best short accounts of life and social conditions during the age of Shakespeare are given by Salzman in his *English Life under the Tudors* (O.U.P., 1937), and by M. Byrne in his *Elizabethan Life in Town and Country* (Houghton Mifflin, 1934). *Shakespeare's England* (O.U.P., 1916) is a scholarly compilation containing chapters upon every phase of Elizabethan life, all written with especial attention to Shakespeare's plays. Finally, F. S. Boas's *Introduction to Tudor Drama* (O.U.P., 1933) is a volume written for the reader who, without special knowledge, wishes to understand the dramatic conditions which had their flowering in Shakespeare.

General critical commentaries on Shakespeare's plays
Of the numerous works of Shakespearian criticism, the most interesting and informative are B. Matthew's *Shakespeare as a Playwright*

(Scribners, 1913), George Baker's *The Development of Shakespeare as a Dramatist* (Macmillan, 1907) and M. R. Ridley's *Shakespeare's Plays: A Commentary* (Dutton, 1938).

Criticism on *Henry IV, Part II*

Shakespeare's use of the historical background is fully discussed by Lily B. Campbell in *Shakespeare's Histories* (The Huntington Library, 1947). Less readable, but extremely thought-provoking is the chapter on Henry V in *Political Characters of Shakespeare* by John Palmer (Macmillan, 1945), while the factual basis of the play is examined by E. M. W. Tillyard in his *Shakespeare's History Plays* (Chatto and Windus, 1944). Finally, the student can do no better than refer to H. N. Hudson's *Shakespeare's Characters*, Vol. II, chapter three (Ginn, Heath & Co).